EDMUND RICE

Knock
14/4/02

Edmund Rice
1762–1844

DÁIRE KEOGH

FOUR COURTS PRESS

Set in 10 on 12 point Ehrhardt
and published by
FOUR COURTS PRESS
Kill Lane, Blackrock, Co. Dublin, Ireland
and in North America by
FOUR COURTS PRESS
c/o ISBS, 5804 NE Hassalo Street, Portland, OR 97213.

A catalogue record for this title
is available from the British Library.

ISBN 1-85182-211-9

Printed in Ireland
by Colour Books Ltd, Dublin.

For the Brothers and Teachers of Synge Street School

Contents

Illustrations

Preface

The forthcoming beatification of Edmund Rice will undoubtedly stimulate debate on his contribution to the development of modern Irish Catholicism. He is perhaps one of the best known men of his generation, yet one about whom least is known. For this reason, I have attempted to bring together the various contemporary accounts and place them in the dynamic context of period.

I am especially indebted to the trojan work of Br M.C. Normoyle, who has edited Rice's correspondence and written his most thorough biography, *A Tree is Planted* (1976), published privately by the Christian Brothers. I want also to thank Br A.M. McDonnell, Provincial of St Helen's province, and Br Michael Murray for all their assistance.

I am grateful too, for the encouragement received from colleagues and friends: David Dickson, Berna Fahy, Hugh Fenning, Bill King, Jim McElroy, Séamus McPhillips, F.X. Martin, Niall Ó Ciosáin and John O'Shea. Especial thanks to James Kelly and Kevin Whelan for reading and commenting on draft chapters. Finally, thanks must go to Michael Adams, Martin Fanning and Ronan Gallagher of Four Courts Press.

I

Spring

In her well known study of eighteenth-century Ireland, Edith Mary Johnston utilises an elegant phrase to describe the period; 'for the elite [it was] an age of elegance, and for every section of the community an age of insecurity'.[1] The century was born from the embers of the Williamite Wars: while the Catholic Jacobites had been defeated, the Protestant community was left with a very real sense of its own insecurity. Fear became an obsession and it was within this context that the penal laws were enacted to protect the Protestant interest.

I

Raised on the memories and lore of the Ulster rebellion and massacres of 1641, Irish Protestants believed that they remained dangerously exposed to the threat of a renewed attack from a formidable Catholic enemy, at home and abroad. At the root of these fears lay the terms of the Treaty of Limerick (1691) which concluded the wars, but which left the defeated Catholics in a far stronger position than might have been expected. The implications were clear—Catholic strength implied Protestant weakness and there could be no accommodation between the two. The Protestant nation owed its very life to the destruction of Catholic power; as the Church of Ireland archbishop of Dublin, William King, put it 'either they or we must be ruined'. It is against this pervasive background of fear that the penal laws must be set.

Rather than reflecting Protestant triumphalism or a desire for revenge, the penal laws illustrate their deep felt insecurity. It was this emotion which prompted the introduction of two bills in 1695—the first of the penal laws—forbidding Catholics from keeping arms or a horse worth more than £5. Both of these measures had strict military objectives and it is the reactionary nature of these and subsequent laws which gave the 'Popery code' its uneven character. One recent historian has argued that, far from being a systematic 'code', the penal legislation against Catholics was, in fact, 'a rag bag of measures enacted piecemeal over half a century in response to a variety of immediate pressures and grievances'.[3]

The penal laws, then, are best understood as an attempt by the Protestant state to curb the growth of 'popery', the dangerous political system which Catholicism represented, not the Catholic religion as such. In an eighteenth-century context, land lay at the base of all political power, so the harshest of the penal laws were directed against Catholic property. The 1704 Act 'to prevent the further growth of popery' (2. Ann, c. 6) represented a formidable challenge to Catholic landowners. The Act reflected Protestant insecurity and attempted to accomplish the destruction of the Catholic landed interest which the Treaty of Limerick had left largely intact.

The 1704 Act prohibited a Catholic from buying land or leasing it for more than thirty-one years; leases of the permitted length had to be held at a prohibitive rent of at least two-thirds of the yearly value. Existing Catholic estates were to be dismantled by the notorious gavelling clause which demanded the division of the estate on the death of the proprietor, unless the eldest son conformed to the established Church, in which case he would inherit the entire holding. If, however, the son conformed during the father's lifetime, the father became his tenant for life.

Under the impact of this legislation, Catholic land ownership was greatly reduced. In 1703, Catholics held an estimated fourteen per cent of the land, while the traveller Arthur Young believed that the figure had fallen to five per cent by 1776. On the surface, these figures reflect a dramatic reduction in Catholic fortunes and have traditionally been accepted as evidence of the success of the penal laws. These figures, however, need qualification. Recent research has emphasised the degree to which Catholics could rely on trustees; conformity to the established Church was very often nominal and there existed a large 'convert interest' of land owning families like the Brownes, the Lynches and the Dalys, with Catholic relatives and sympathies.[4]

A distinction must also be made between ownership and leasehold: when property in the form of leasehold and livestock is taken into account, it has been estimated that Catholic personal property amounted to half the total by the end of the eighteenth-century. No concerted effort was made to exclude Catholics from trade, especially the provisions trade, and in time they came to possess economic strength in the commercial and professional middle classes, particularly in Munster and Leinster.[5] It is a combination of factors like these which explain the prosperity of the Rices of Westcourt.

The purpose of the religious aspects of the penal code remain uncertain. On one hand, it is argued that the laws intended that the whole nation would be Protestant, but this could hardly be the case, since such a move would dilute the Protestant profile and loosen their grip on their jealously guarded power.[6] Therefore, because the primary concern of the penal code was with property, there were large and never resolved ambiguities when it came to religious practice.[7] Measures against clerics and worship were contained in the Banishment Act of 1697 (9 William III, c. 1), the 1704 Act 'to prevent the further growth of popery' and the Registration Act of the same year (2 Ann, c. 7).

Had the terms of the Banishment Act, which was aimed at bishops and regular clergy, been strenuously implemented, the Catholic clergy in Ireland would have died out in time; there could be no ordinations without bishops, and the entry of priests from abroad was forbidden. Four hundred and twenty-four regular priests were transported in 1698, mainly to France. Many more remained in Ireland passing themselves off as secular clergy, while others returned once the initial commotion had died down. The position of the Catholic hierarchy in 1698 was already extremely weak. There were no more than eight bishops in the country and three of these left under the terms of the Act.

Parish clergy were not affected by the laws but in 1704 they were compelled to appear before the court of sessions, register their name, address, age, parish, date and place of ordination and the name of the ordaining prelate. Priests were confined to their own county, forbidden from keeping a curate, and obliged to present two securities of £50 to guarantee their 'good behaviour'. The Act, under which almost eleven hundred priests registered, had the effect of granting legal recognition to the Catholic diocesan clergy and, far from leading to the extinction of the church, actually facilitated its re-emergence. Priests were free to say Mass and administer the sacraments, churches remained open, and the act contained sufficient loopholes to allow for creative exploitation, often with the collusion of compliant magistrates. Many regulars—members of religious orders registered as diocesan clergy and bishops as parish priests, so that by Queen Anne's death in 1714 there were fourteen bishops in Ireland. The returns made in the 1731 'Report on the state of popery' reflect the failure of the laws; almost every diocese had a bishop, clerical numbers had risen, Mass houses continued to be built and a rudimentary educational system was in place.[8]

Educational restrictions were among the first penal laws put in place. As early as 1695, it was enacted that 'no person of the popish religion may publicly teach school or instruct youth', but politically the most important provision of the act was the clause which aimed to stem the flow of students going to the continent. The purpose of this law was to limit contact between Irish Catholics and their continental allies—the title of the measure was 'An act to restrain foreign education'.[9] Rather than intending to condemn Catholic youth to ignorance, the penal laws attempted to secure a Protestant control over education by curbing the potentially political influence of the schoolmaster.

In 1731 the Church of Ireland primate, Englishman Hugh Boulter, extended the scope of government education measures by giving them an evangelical character. He founded a society for establishing primary schools whose aim was 'that the children of the popish and other poor natives ... may be instructed in the English tongue and in the principles of true religion and loyalty'. The scheme received the royal charter in 1733 and was initially financed by individual benefactors and a royal bounty of £1000 per year. In addition, the Irish parliament voted it the proceeds of a tax on hawkers and pedlars in 1745 and these grants were considerably increased from 1757.[10] The foundation of these Charter Schools led to an over-reaction on the Catholic side about their potential for proselytism. While historians would agree that this new departure was a face-saving measure on behalf of the government, an admission that the Protestants would remain a minority in Ireland, they did force the Catholics to examine their own educational provisions. This led to a rapid increase in the number of Catholic parish schools which taught basic skills and gave catechetical instruction.[11]

Overall then, while there were incidents of priest hunting and cases of transportation, by and large, attempts to implement the penal laws in the early decades of the eighteenth-century were sporadic, with Ulster suffering most. The laws remained on the statute books and hung in suspended animation over the heads of the Catholic clergy to be revived at moments of international crisis or perceived domestic threat, as in the years 1715, 1720, 1745, and during the war of the Austrian Succession (1740–8) or the Seven Years' War (1756–63). Luke Gardiner, the younger, described the position in a speech to the Irish House of Commons in 1782, when he said that 'the papists were safe from the penal laws so long as the generous and merciful disposition of their countrymen disdained to put them into execution'.[12] The great Edmund Burke, reflecting on such sentiments, declared 'connivance is the relaxation of slavery, not the definition of liberty'.

II

By the accession of George III in 1760, two years before Edmund Rice was born, the Hanoverian dynasty was secure on the throne. The refusal of the Holy See to recognise Charles Edward, on the death of the Old Pretender in 1766, marked the end of the Stuart cause and removed a great deal of suspicion of Catholic loyalty. Rogers, in his history of the Volunteers, traced the rise of the Catholic Church 'from the catacombs' to the 1760s; more recently, Whelan has placed the 'Tridentine surge' in the following decade.[13] Certainly, contemporary travellers such as Arthur Young and Thomas Campbell, were struck by the vitality of the Catholic Church in the 1770s.[14]

Estimates of clerical numbers are incomplete, the most comprehensive figures being those of 1731 and the returns made by the hierarchy to Lord Castlereagh's enquiries in December 1800.[15] In 1731, it was estimated that there were 1445 priests in Ireland of which it was assumed that 700 were members of religious orders. Seventy years later, the numbers of priests had risen to 1800, of whom 400 were regulars. It was frequently claimed in the first half of the eighteenth century that the population could not support large numbers of clergy, but by 1800 there was a universal complaint amongst bishops of a shortage of priests. The figures for that year must be adjusted to allow for the large number of clerics forced to return to Ireland during the French Revolution and the shortage of priests in the period 1795–1812 was caused by the closure of the continental colleges, especially in Paris. Nevertheless, analysis of the available figures points to a decreasing clergy:people ratio. The population of Ireland increased by about eighty eight percent between 1731 and 1800, whereas the number of priests rose by a mere twelve percent. This translates roughly to one priest for every 1587 Catholics in 1731, compared to one to every 2676 at the end of the century.[16] There were, inevitably, great regional variations. In Ossory, Bishops Burke, Troy and Lanigan constantly complained of a shortage of priests. While Troy had ordained twenty three priests between 1778 and 1785, there were scarcely sixty priests in the diocese by 1792, but this still allowed for a ratio of one priest to every 1600 Catholics.[17]

The dislocation caused by the penal laws inevitably led to a weakening of institutional structures within the Church. Many abuses did exist, such as those recorded in the early visitations of Bishop Nicholas Sweetman of Ferns in the 1750s and the shortcomings recorded by Patrick Plunket on his first tour of his Meath diocese thirty years later.[18] At Kilskeer, in the barony of Upper Kells, Plunket reported:

> The altar step, and the place about the altar, by no means clean or orderly. The crucifix too bad. A cruet or small phial for the wine absolutely wanting. The chapel not closed, and therefore exposed to dirt and profanation. A clerk absolutely necessary to keep up some little decency in the house of God.

In almost every parish, Plunket complained of the poor quality of the vestments and sacred vessels and the irregularity of the sanctuary. Of greater concern to him were the heterodox liturgical practices of priests who failed to preach on Sunday or who were ignorant of the decrees of the Council of Trent. At the parish of Turin, Plunket wryly commented that 'every face seemed to wear visible marks of dissatisfaction at the pastor's unpastoral conduct'.[19]

Plunket's dissatisfaction, and the demands he made upon his clergy, reflect the renewed vigour of the episcopacy in the later eighteenth-century. Throughout the country, younger bishops engaged in regular visitations of their dioceses; many parishes were visited annually and complaints wrere carefully investigated. The ignorance of the laity was a grave concern and Mass attendance was often low. Congregations showed little respect and it was common for bishops to refuse confirmation on account of poor preparation. The emphasis placed on catechesis is reflected in almost every episcopal report to Rome, in the period 1782–1803; in the absence of adequate schools, the Confraternity of Christian Doctrine was established in most dioceses to assist in this task. A considerable amount of religious and devotional material was printed for an eager readership; by 1782, Archbishop James Butler's 'General Catechism' had gone through eleven editions since its publication in 1775.[20] Greater devotion to the Eucharist was promoted by the Archconfraternity of the Blessed Sacrament, and sodalities of the rosary and scapular, introduced by the regulars in the 1720s, were widely established.

Episcopal efforts were made to regulate religious practice. Plunket's visitation diary for 1780 reveals that many parishes followed incomplete liturgical calendars; in 1775, Dr John Carpenter, archbishop of Dublin, employed John Morris to print a new missal containing the feasts of all the saints of Ireland. Plunket recommended this missal—believed by Carpenter to have been the first printed in these islands—to his clergy.[21] The keeping of parochial registers began in earnest and renewed efforts were made to stem the abuses the hierarchy associated with wakes and patterns, which formed a major feature of the religious and social life for the laity in the late eighteenth century. Amhlaoidh Ó Súilleabháin's description of the pattern at St James' Well, in Rice's Callan, in 1829 illustrates their potential for abuse:

> There were gooseberries and currants and cherries for the children: ginger bread for grown girls: strong beer, and maddening whiskey for wranglers and busybodies: open-doored booths filled with lovers: bag-pipers, and 'riosp-raspers' [fiddlers] making music there for young folks: and pious pilgrims making their stations around the well. My children and myself left the Well at six o clock.[22]

The most energetic and reforming bishops convened diocesan conferences, through which they attempted to renew their clergy. One day conferences were held between the months of April and October in many dioceses and fines were imposed on those absent without reason. Bishop John Troy revived the conferences in Edmund Rice's home diocese of

Ossory in 1780. These provided a model which many of his confrères followed. Troy chose a theme for each year, and the surviving Dublin plan for 1790 reflects his meticulous approach:

January	Paschal communion—can it be deferred?
February	Viaticum for children and Mass stipends.
March	Why hear Mass, the altar and vestments.
April	The ceremony of the Mass, its language, can it be said in the vernacular?
June	Penance, what is it? Is it necessary, is it a true sacrament of the New Law?
July	Matter for penance and contrition.
August	Sacramental confession.
September	Is contrition necessary only for mortal sins?
October	The minister of penance.
November	Reserved cases, who has faculties to absolve them?
December	The sign of confession.[23]

The Catholic revival was also reflected in the spate of chapel building which characterised the last quarter of the eighteenth-century. The re-emergence of Catholicism was uneven in geographical terms. Broadly it began in mid-Munster/south Leinster and percolated only slowly into Ulster/north Connacht. Contrary to the received image, Catholicism as an institutional force was more firmly established in the richer areas, the upper social classes and the towns. The regional pattern was reflected in the building of new churches.[24] The older chapels had become symbols of backwardness in the eyes of the hierarchy and the Catholic middle class. They expressed their confidence and aspirations through a massive programme of church building which continued into the nineteenth century. In 1766, Alexander McAuley commented on the changes in Ulster:

> Till within these few years, there was scarce a Mass house to be seen in the northern counties of Ulster. Now Mass houses are spreading over most parts of the country. Convents, till of late were hid in corners. Now they are openly avowed in the very metropolis. From the Revolution till a few years ago, Mass houses were little huts in remote and obscure places. Now they are sumptuous buildings in the most public and conspicuous places.[25]

'Sumptuous' was certainly an exaggeration, but few contemporaries failed to be impressed by the material improvement of chapel buildings. The penal chapels of the seventeenth and eighteenth-centuries were basic and the descriptions contained in Bishop Plunket's visitation diary reflects the material poverty of the Church. The older rural chapels were generally between fifty and sixty feet long and half as wide, with a mud floor and a low, thatched roof. It was a barn like structure, with a whitewashed mud or stone walls, a window on either side of a simple raised altar and one door at the back of the chapel. There were no galleries or furnishings, congregations stood or knelt during Mass, and the chapel was almost without decoration, apart from a crucifix behind the altar.[26]

The penal Mass house, *teach an phobail*, was the focal point of the community, serving as church, school, and meeting place; on occasion it was used for threshing corn. The new churches, or barn chapels of the late penal years, were grander in scale, built of stone and with a pitched, slated roof; steeples and bells were, however, still forbidden under the penal laws. The chapels remained simple in decoration, but efforts were made to improve the sanctuary, the altar and the quality of the vestments and altar plate. From the barn plan, they evolved to an L-shape and the more common cruciform plan. Floors were generally flagged, and galleries, often with pews, accommodated the larger congregations.[27] Yet, even these were proving inadequate given the larger Catholic population and the more elaborate scale of public liturgies. The consecration of Bishop James Lanigan of Ossory in Kilkenny 1789 reflects the level to which the Catholic establishment had emerged from the restrictions of the penal era. Three bishops were present in the sanctuary along with seventy two priests. One witness remarked that 'the chapel was so crowded that the gallery began to give warning of some danger'.[28]

The level of building is recorded in the episcopal *relationes status* sent to Rome. In Munster, where church building proceeded faster than elsewhere, Bishop Matthew McKenna built eleven new churches in Cloyne in the ten years after 1775 and James Butler II spent one thousand guineas building a house and improving the church in Thurles. Francis Moylan boasted that the churches of Tralee and Killarney, which he had built, surpassed any Protestant church in the diocese in size and workmanship.[29] The scale of the cathedrals in Waterford (1793) and Cork (1799) spoke volumes about Catholic confidence and pretensions. More than this, the new cathedrals were a witness to the re-emergence of the Catholic hierarchy. Episcopal communications in the early decades of the century were sourced '*in loco refugii nostri*', but, though penal legislation was still in place until the early 1790s, the bishops now addressed their flocks from their seat, often conspicuously re-established in the principal town of the diocese.

Politically, too, the Catholic laity made considerable advances as 'between 1774 and 1795 the legal position of Catholics in Irish society was so transformed as to merit the use of the word 'revolution'.[30] From 1760 onwards, a formal Catholic Committee had led an undistinguished campaign for relief from the disabilities of the penal laws. For the first twenty years of its existence, repeated declarations of loyalty met with little success, but Catholics were fortunate in that a combination of events prompted the British ministry to rethink its position on Catholic relief. On one level, there were tensions in the Anglo-Irish relationship, but there was also a softening of anti-Catholic opinion at an elite level in England. Of more immediate importance, perhaps, were the military requirements of the empire.[31]

These considerations, then, rather than the campaign of the Catholic Committee prompted the Relief Acts of 1778 and 1782. The first of these measures, introduced by Luke Gardiner, formed part of the government's recruitment drive in the context of the American War. The Act dealt almost exclusively with landed property; it allowed Catholics hold land on equal terms with Protestants and the hated gavelling law was removed. Ultimately the significance of the act lay not so much in its content as in its principles, which Edmund Burke correctly predicted would 'extend further' in time. Forty years later, in the wake of O'Connell's 'revolution', Thomas Wyse vindicated Burke's confidence, arguing that Gardiner's Relief Act 'was the first step which really emancipated'.[32]

The 1778 relief measures left intact all the restrictions on the Catholic clergy and worship, but the momentum for change was still in place. With the initiative coming from London, Catholic loyalty proved a trump card in the face of increasing Volunteer pressure on the administration. Towards the end of the War in 1782, the government sponsored a second relief act in an effort to detach Catholics from their flirtation with the Volunteers. Gardiner's second relief act was much more sweeping than the first. The remaining disabilities relating to land were removed and the secular clergy were freed to perform ecclesiastical functions, though they were still prohibited from assuming ecclesiastical rank or titles, or to minister in a church with a steeple or bell. A prohibition was placed on the future entry of members of religious orders into Ireland but this was merely a re-enactment of an existing statute which had long been in disuse. Except for an obligation to take the Test Oath, no measures were to be taken against regulars already in the country. The Act also allowed the establishment of Catholic schools, on receipt of a licence from the Protestant ordinary, but endowment of such schools was forbidden.

The easy passage of the 1782 Relief Act through parliament brought an effective end to the penal laws in so far as they had restricted Catholic worship in Ireland for almost a century. Certain civil disabilities were still in place—the major professions and political rights were withheld—but in time these became the goal of a radicalised political campaign in which the Waterford merchant Edmund Rice played his part.

2

Callan

'Walk through any town in Ireland, but run through Callan'. In the late eighteenth-century, Callan was known as *Calainn a Clampair*, or 'Wrangling Callan', and not without reason.[1] Tension characterised the town and these pressures illustrate the immense complexity of the society which fails to surface in Daniel Corkery's schematic *Hidden Ireland*.[2] Far from the accepted notions of the conflict between 'big-house' and the great mass outside the gate, it was there that the real struggle took place as Catholics jostled for position in a rapidly evolving society. In the case of the Rices of Westcourt, we can see many of the intricacies of the penal era which challenge the accepted images of Catholics smarting under unrelenting persecution. Instead, it is possible to construct a picture of a resilient community, not merely adapting to their situation but, displaying creativity and confidence in the face of varying degrees of opposition.

I

Callan is situated on the King's River, a tributary of the River Nore, ten miles south-west of Kilkenny and two miles from the Tipperary border. The Anglo-Norman town of Callan was founded by William Marshall and received its charter in 1207. Documentary evidence for eighteenth-century Callan is scarce, but the English traveller Rufus Chetwood has left us a fine description of the town in 1748:

> This place seems to lie in the ruins Oliver [Cromwell] left it. You see the remains of three castles, and an old church of the Gothic building [old St Mary's] on the right as you enter the town, but the roof is gone and all the rest a mere anatomy ... The situation of this place is very agreeable, upon a stream called the King's River, dividing in two branches above the town ... The main stream runs under a bridge of four arches, and the small one (after driving a mill) under two ... Upon this stream about a mile below Callan, is a very famous iron mill, that brings great profit to the proprietors. The town is built in the form of a cross, and in the centre a cross

is erected, with a square glass lantern, that gives light in the night to travellers that come from the four cardinal points of the compass. One would imagine this town should be in a more thriving condition since the two great roads of Cork and Limerick go through it.[3]

The economic condition of the town declined as the century progressed and its poverty was reflected in the quality of housing; of a total of 530 dwellings in 1800, only 39 paid hearth tax and 46 window tax.[4] Few enjoyed the comfort of a bed; writing in 1801, William Tighe commented that 'a pallet to sleep on is a comfort unknown .. a wad of straw or perhaps heath laid on a damp clay floor forms their resting place'.[5] The population of the civil parish increased rapidly, from thirteen hundred in 1731 to around three and a half thousand by the end of the century. There were few employment prospects: the iron mill closed in 1788 on account of a timber shortage and the expansion of James Agar's weaving industry never matched expectations. In 1845 the *Parliamentary Gazetteer* described the town as 'the very impersonation of Irish poverty and wretchedness'.[6] With such bleak prospects, many had no option but to join the significant numbers emigrating to Newfoundland.

Whatever prosperity Callan enjoyed arose out of its role as a parliamentary borough and market town for the surrounding countryside. There were two market days per week, Wednesday and Saturday, and three fairs were held annually; in 1790 that number was increased to four. The local schoolmaster/shop-keeper Amhlaoidh Ó Súilleabháin has left us an account of one undistinguished fair day in 1827:

Callan Abbey

A bright sunny morning: a bracing south-west wind: seven o clock, the clouds lying on the mountains: the day growing dark: two cows and nine or ten pigs on the fair green: a tent being put up: eleven o clock, small pigs dear being sent to England: sucking pigs dear: if a low price were asked for a yearling it could be sold: no demand for any other kind of cattle: plenty of calves and yearlings there, but little demand for them ... little business at the one tent which is on the fair green: no business being done by the small traders, alas! 'Better crossness than loneliness.' It is a 'mock-fair' unquestionably.[7]

Callan lay in the centre of some of the richest farmland in Ireland. We have already noted the distinctions which must be made when discussing the question of Catholic land holdings during the penal era. Catholics could avoid the rigorous application of the law by relying on trustees, nominal conversion and the presence of large 'convert interest' of land owning families with Catholic relatives and sympathies. In this sense, conversions to the established Church reinforced, rather than weakened, the Catholic position. Catholics relied on this group, not only on the land, but in parliament where sympathetic members like Lucius O'Brien, Anthony Malone and Edmund Burke defended their cause.[8]

Nowhere were the implications of this survival more clearly visible than in south Tipperary and south Kilkenny.[9] A large portion of the land in these counties remained in Catholic hands due to the sympathetic influence of the Ormonde family and the Catholic Butlers who had benefited from the terms of the Treaty of Limerick. This Catholic branch of the family owned considerable land in county Tipperary, especially the large estate at Cahir and another at Kilcash. The survival of these Catholic or crypto-Catholic landlords was especially significant in maintaining Catholic land holdings. On the Cahir estate alone, in the period 1720–50, 97 of 141 leases were to Catholics like the Sheehys, Nagles and Prendergasts.[10]

These prosperous families, middlemen farmers engaged in grazing and dairying, were vital in the preservation of the Gaelic culture celebrated by the Munster poets of the eighteenth-century. They were, according to Whelan, 'the tradition bearers, who survived *in situ* through national upheavals to provide the backbone of a cohesive, if secretive, culture'.[11] In Callan the leading Catholic families were the Butlers of Westcourt Castle (the old Manor house of Callan) and the Smyths of Damagh, who lived in Callan Lodge which they had acquired in the 1730s. Beneath the subgentry there was a layer of strong farmers who had advanced socially from the small-farm ranks in the expansionist economy of the eighteenth-century. Included in this group were the Rices of Westcourt.

The Rices had no great social standing among the old families of county Kilkenny. The earliest references to the Rices in Callan appear in the hearth tax rolls for 1665–6, where John Rys and Patrick, Richard and James Rice appear in the townland of Sunhill. Edmund Rice's father, Robert, had a farm of 182 acres, fifty five of which were at Westcourt and the remaining 127 at Ballykeefe.[12] The Rices were notoriously ambitious and made every effort to consolidate and enlarge this holding, even when this verged on land grabbing. Among the recollections collected for Edmund Rice's cause for canonisation several comment on this fact. The Rices, apparently, were 'ambitious for land and were anxious to get rich quick'. Another recollection claimed that they 'were considered to have been perhaps, endowed by a too keen sense of business' and again that 'they were fond of land and were always anxious to secure a good place'.[13]

The Rice home at Westcourt was similar to many owned by their class. It was a long, low cottage with a deep thatch. It had four bedrooms, each ten feet by nine, a parlour and kitchen, both seventeen feet by twelve, and a hall way. In keeping with most large Catholic farmers, their lifestyle was frugal. In 1802, William Tighe remarked on the simplicity of the prosperous Aylward family:

> They slaughter their pigs generally at home and eat the offal which is the only animal food they usually make use of, living principally on potatoes and some griddle bread. Their incomes are probably not less than £600 or £700 a year.[14]

Yet, this modest lifestyle and frugality was in part the key to the strength of these rising families. With small outgoings, the families were able to endure hard times, and during the agricultural boom in the last quarter of the century they were in a position to accumulate capital. As the penal laws were dismantled from 1778 onwards, the Catholics availed of leases, often outbidding their more ostentatious Protestant neighbours.[15] Capital was also available for education, commercial investment, and the provision of all important dowries.[16]

Strategic marriages formed an important aspect of the Catholic advance. The usual pattern is reflected in the marriage of Edmund's parents, which was an alliance of two rising families. The *Memoirs*, edited by Normoyle record that the Rices were 'related to all the independent farmers in the locality'.[17] Edmund's mother, Margaret, was one of the Tierney's who farmed one hundred acres at Maxtown. Her family were well respected and related to many prominent families, including the Smyths of Damagh and the Mahers of Tipperary. Margaret Tierney was a widow and her marriage to Robert Rice gave him two step-children, Joan and Jane Murphy.

Yet the advance of such large tenant farmers was not made without

Rice's home at Westcourt

serious social consequences and increasing land hunger led to heightened
social tensions which was given expression in Whiteboy activity. Beginning in protest against the enclosure of common land in Tipperary in
1761, the 'levelling' of the Whiteboys eventually spread through much of
Munster and south Leinster where they opposed high rents, evictions
and, above all, the hated tithes paid to the established church.[18] The
Whiteboy activities illustrate clearly the complexity of late eighteenth-
century Irish society. Simple sectarian interpretations cannot be applied to
this movement, since a great deal of its attention was directed against
avaricious Catholic farmers. The bishops of Munster denounced the
Whiteboys in a series of pastorals in the 1760s. In 1774 the archbishop of
Cashel, James Butler II, took measures further, organising the people of
Ballyragget in a league sworn at their chapel by a justice of the peace to
defend their landlord, Robert Butler, brother of the archbishop.[19]

As a result of large scale unemployment, the poor of Callan relied on
the casual and seasonal work available on the farms around. In this they
were forced to compete with the 'spailpin' from the even poorer areas of
the west who trekked across country in search of work. Naturally, their
presence on the labour market was unwelcome and occasional skirmishes
took place in Callan. In time these 'spailpin' became targets for Whiteboy
aggression. Tipperary men working in Ballyragget, Urlingford and Johns-
town were attacked and made swear never to work in Kilkenny again; in
1779 rumours were spread that press gangs were operating at the hiring
fairs in Kilkenny in order to frighten would be labourers from outside the
county.[20] It was against this background that Bishop Troy of Ossory deliv-

ered his gothic excommunication of the Whiteboys in 1775 condemning them to

> everlasting Hell ... When they shall be judged, may they be con-
> demned ... may their posterity be cut off in one generation. Let
> their children be carried about as vagabonds and beg and let them
> be cast out of their dwellings. May the usurers search all their
> substance and let strangers plunder their labours. May there be
> none to help them, nor none to pity their fatherless offspring. May
> their names be blotted out ... let their memory perish from the
> earth. Let all the congregation say Amen, Amen, Amen.[21]

Eleven years later, in August 1786, when the Rightboys intended to administer their oaths in the chapels of the county, the redoubtable Troy
closed the churches of the diocese and the people of Kilkenny went
without Mass.

II

It was into this difficult environment that Edmund Rice was born on 1
June 1762, the fourth of seven sons. Some days later he was baptised in
Callan and given the name of his grandfather. Callan was well served for
churches. The parish church beside the Green was typical of many penal
chapels with its stone walls, trampled clay floor, rustic benches and spartan
altar. The Butler presence ensured a clerical continuity in the town throughout the penal era. As early as 1704 the parish priest used a house belonging to the Ormonde family to offer Mass; in 1766, while Bishop Thomas
Burke complained of clerical shortages in the diocese, there were three
secular priests in Callan.[22]

In addition, the Augustinians had been in the town since 1467.[23] The
friars had a thatched chapel in Clodeen Lane, near the cross, and there
were four members in the community in 1766 but these more than likely
worked in the countryside, questing and attending stations.[24] The friars
had an influential presence in Callan and in 1781 the priory became the
novitiate for the province. The novitiate was opened with Dr Troy's
blessing and the Master had five novices in the first year.[25]

The friars were frequent visitors at Westcourt and the young Edmund
received his early education from one of their number, Patrick Grace. The
'Bráithrín Liath', as he became known on account of his premature grey-
ness, was a wandering schoolmaster before he joined the Order. It was at
this time that he was employed by the Rices to give instruction to their
young children. This young man made an enormous impression on the
boys and it is to his influence that John Rice's vocation to the Augustinians

has been attributed, while the 'well disposed Edmund was deeply moved by his mentor'.[26] The medium of instruction was Irish and it seems certain that the young Edmund was called Éamann at home. The language had was still widely spoken around Kilkenny and Tighe commented in 1802 that during Mass the priests 'preached alternatively in Irish and English, but always in Irish if they were desirous to be well understood'.[27]

Callan was poorly served for schools. For a population of almost three and a half thousand, the town had two schools, one conducted by the Protestant rector and the second a 'hedge school' in Moate Lane. This was a small, one storied building which catered for thirty students at most. One of Rice's earliest followers, Callanman Edmund Grace, has left us a description of the hedge school he attended. While we have no definite evidence, we may surmise that this was the school attended by Rice:

> 'The Academy' ... consisted of a small antique structure covered with a verdant coat of thatch. The door was the only lateral aperture, and the remains of what were once windows were securely closed ... When a new boy presented himself for admission he was approached in somewhat courtly style by the master, a portly man, attired in frieze body-coat, knee-breeches, and woollen stockings, and cordially greeted with the pious salutation, 'God save you'... This established confidence and led to the business part of the reception, during which the aspirant to participation in the benefits of the 'Academy' was informed that the terms were fourpence a week and a half-penny for dancing, which was practised on the door of the 'Academy' laid flat on the clay floor. Thus the door, like Goldsmith's 'bed by night and chest of drawers by day, had 'its double debt to pay'.

Students were taught individually and the greater part of the day was spent 'writing', copying headlines, and 'rehearsing' or learning facts by heart.[28] In time, Edmund graduated to a school in Kilkenny, possibly the predecessor of Burrell's Hall, where the Rices paid £20 per year for their son to receive a grounding in commercial subjects. After a short while, Edmund was apprenticed to his uncle Michael, a prosperous merchant in Waterford.

This then, the Ireland of Rice's boyhood, was the real hidden Ireland. Not the romantic image of the 'big house' surrounded by a mass of undifferentiated poverty, not the 'penal era' of unrelenting persecution, but the age of endurance and emergence. This was a story of survival and opportunity where, in an age of rapid political development, ambitious Catholics were in a position to exploit the many occasions which arose.

3

Merchant

When Edmund Rice made his way to Waterford in 1779, there was no bridge across the Suir. The young apprentice stood on the Kilkenny side of the river and waited for the ferry which carried him the distance to his new life beyond. The next twenty years were to be the most eventful in his life; these years brought him commercial success beyond expectation. They also brought unforeseen personal tragedy which changed the course of his life. His was a classic conversion experience, not dramatic in the sense of St Paul's, but these years were marked by a number of well-defined steps which chart his transition from merchant to founder.[1]

I

The agricultural boom in commercial tillage and dairying in the second half of the eighteenth-century brought prosperity to the south-east. Waterford was ideally placed to reap the benefits of this economic miracle. A great deal of the agricultural surplus of the rich lands of its hinterland were shipped along the Suir, the Nore and the Barrow to be processed in the city. Waterford developed flour-milling, brewing, distilling, bacon-curing, tanning, soap making and other industries whose products were exported through its fine port. These goods went to England, Spain and Portugal, but fortunes were also made servicing the triangular trade with the West Indies and North America.

By the middle of the century, the port was thriving, to an extent where it rivalled Cork in the colonial trade; Smith has left a dramatic impression of this vibrant city:

> The Quay is about half a mile in length and of considerable breadth, not inferior to but rather exceeds the most celebrated in Europe. To it the largest trading vessels may conveniently come up, both to load and to unload, and at a small distance opposite it may lie and constantly afloat. The Exchange, Custom House and other public buildings, ranged along the quay are no small addition to its beauty, which together with a number of shipping afford an agreeable pros-

pect. The whole is fronted with hewn stone, well paved and in some places it is forty feet broad. To it are built five moles or piers which stretch forward; at the pier heads ships of 500 tons may load and unload and lie afloat. In the road before the Quay the river is between four and five fathoms deep at low water where sixty sail of ship may ride conveniently, clear of each other in clean ground.[2]

The prosperity of the last decades of the century brought further expansion. The French Wars, too, increased trade. Between 1790 and 1810 it is estimated that as many as 1000 ships, averaging 900 tons each, visited the port annually. In addition, Waterford had a fishing fleet of eighty vessels which gave rise to a local fish-curing industry.[3]

The Rices shared in the prosperity of Waterford where Catholics made up one-third of the merchant numbers.[4] Michael Rice had a thriving provisioning business near the Quay and engaged in extensive home and foreign trade. Rice appears to have specialised in livestock, slaughtering, packing and exporting meat to Bristol. In addition he had lucrative contracts with the army, the Admiralty and shipping companies. A significant portion of his trade was with Newfoundland; exporting meat and importing the dried 'lander' fish which formed an important part of the Waterford diet.[5] In 1788 Edmund was joined in Waterford by his younger brother John. Having learned the details of the export trade, he was sent to Cadiz to oversee the Spanish section of the business.

The mobility of families like the Rices in the south-east is quite remarkable. Cullen believes that it is not present on such a scale in any other part of Ireland, outside the Presbyterian community of the north. He attributes this to a 'a combination of social pressures and aspirations which predisposed even the lower classes to mobility'. An illustration of this is the annual migration of as many as 5000 individuals for seasonal labour in Newfoundland.[6] A more recent commentator has identified this mobility as a crucial part of Catholic re-emergence. Kevin Whelan has pointed to essential links between the surviving gentry/strong farmers group and their co-religionists in the towns. He identifies a 'synchronisation of zones', reflected in 'the symbiosis of town and country ... the integration of marriage fields and the constant replenishment of town families by rural recruits'.[7] All of these features are illustrated in the case of Edmund Rice.

II

We have few recollections of Rice from this time. One of the earliest descriptions comes from Austin Dunphy, later one of his disciples:

The first time I saw him was in 1796. He was then a very fine looking man, and had a high character among the Catholic people and mercantile classes of the country. Indeed, he was respected and trusted by men of all creeds and classes.

He was above middle height, being about six feet, of sanguine complexion, with eyes large and expressive, and of a bright hazel colour.

His frame of body was formed for active habits, and his intellectual powers were of a high order. He had broad and just views of life and its varied problems, and possessed great mental vigour and steadfastness of purpose. He was generous, warm-hearted, and most paternal.[8]

Almost every recollection refers to his keen business sense while others mention his wit and humour. All are agreed on his devotion to prayer and colleagues recalled how he would say the rosary as he travelled the roads to markets and fairs. If there was one criticism of him in this period, it was that he was 'too fastidious about his dress'.[9]

Edmund's business connections introduced him to a bustling social circle. Friendships included the Aylward and St Leger families; Edward Shiel, who had amassed a fortune in Cadiz, and his son, politician and Catholic activist, Richard Lalor Shiel. Fr John Power, parish priest of St Johns and future bishop of Waterford and Lismore, was to be an influential friend. Rice had also a close friendship with the poet Tadhg Gaelach Ó Súilleabháin, whom he met in the 'Yellow House' on the Lacken Road. This is a significant friendship, both in terms of Edmund Rice's participation in the Gaelic survival of Munster, but also on account of Tadhg Gaelach's religious conversion, reflected in his *Pious Miscellany*.

It was at this time, too, that Edmund met Mary Elliott, the daughter of a Waterford tanner, whom he married in 1785. Very little is known about her, or indeed about this important episode in his life; the first time she is named is in the *Memoir* of Martin O'Flynn collected one hundred and sixty years after her death. McCarthy's biography of Edmund Rice which runs to five hundred and thirty five pages treats the marriage in one paragraph. The absence of information is curtly excused by the fact that 'the early brothers, with a delicacy of feeling which is commendable, seldom refer to it'! The marriage, of which regrettably we know so little, ended with her tragic death in January 1789, leaving Edmund a twenty-seven year old widower and father of a handicapped daughter. Again, perhaps reflecting Edmund's own reticence, nothing is known of the event save for the brief detail contained in the *Dublin Evening Post*: 'Died at Ballybricken the wife of Mr Rice'.

Family tradition, related by Sr Josephine Rice of St John's Newfoundland in 1929, holds that Mrs Rice died in a riding accident:

> The Founder had been married to a lady of a well-to-do family who was fond of the hunt as most wealthy people were in those days. When she was well-advanced with child, she was riding and was thrown from her horse, dying as a result of the accident. The doctor managed to save the child who had evidently been injured by the fall and hence did not develop normally. This was the child he provided for when he began his work.[13]

This account has been convincingly challenged by Liam Ó Caithnia.[14] As a folklorist he questioned the reliability of the transcription: why would Sr Josephine refer to Edmund Rice as 'The Founder'? Apart from this and other textual criticisms, he speculates on how this tradition could be preserved for one hundred and forty years by the Newfoundland Rices when not one of the 250 interviews contained in Normoyle's *Memoirs* refer to the event? Ó Caithnia rejects this riding accident thesis and instead accepts the tradition that Mary Rice died in the fever which swept Europe in 1789: that 'dreadful fever' which Dorothea Herbert claimed, 'raged all over the World ... and carried off Millions in every quarter of the Globe'.[15]

Little is known, also, about the extent of Mary Rice's handicap. Several of the memoirs refer to the fact that she was 'delicate'. Ó Caithnia believes that the story of the fall is more correctly related to the child's condition and not the mother's death. Similar motifs were often invoked to account for handicap or mental weakness in order to protect 'the *good name* of the family'.[16] Edmund cared for his daughter in Waterford and when he embarked on his mission he entrusted her to his brother Patrick. In later years he made financial provision for her welfare; in 1826 accounts reveal that she was boarded out at a considerable expense of £16 per annum.

Payments for her support were made from Mount Sion up until 1849; when these were queried, Brother Ignatius Kelly replied 'if it were that weak-headed creature the D......r, I would feel bound to support her'. Payments continued, generally through the director of the Carrick community, until July 1858 when a note was entered in the account book: 'M. Rice, who from time to time received something for her maintenance, died at Carrick-on-Suir on 23rd day of January 1859, and was buried in the churchyard at Carrickbeg, January 24th, '59'.[17]

III

Edmund's desolation at the death of his wife can hardly be imagined. Of a friend in similar circumstances he later wrote, 'may the Lord help her, she is now [in] the dregs of misery and misfortune. I pity the poor Mother, it will break her heart'.[18] Yet this double tragedy was to play an enormous part in his conversion and from this period it is possible to identify an increased religious and social consciousness.

We have already noted the 'Tridentine surge' which took place in the last decades of the eighteenth-century. This was manifested in many ways, chapel building being perhaps the most obvious including the Cathedral of Waterford completed in 1796 at a cost of £20,000. There were, however, more dynamic aspects of this renewal and these were reflected in the increased levels of devotional printing and the growth of confraternities. Edmund Rice was part of this revival. About the year 1790 he joined a number of young men in Waterford who formed a society committed to living more active Christian lives. Among the various duties they promoted was the practice of charity and the frequent reception of the sacraments of the Eucharist and Reconciliation. This was a radical commitment, since frequent reception of the sacrament was uncommon and not particularly stressed by the church until the pontificate of Pius X in our own century.

Edmund's name also appears on subscription lists for several religious imprints, including a 1793 Waterford edition of *The Spiritual Combat*, a translation of Lorenzo Scupoli's classic devotional work. This was to be an influential text and its importance at this stage of Edmund Rice's spiritual development can hardly be over-estimated. One commentator has observed 'he now had to hand an approved manual of perfection which provided a methodical approach to the spiritual life congenial to his ordered business mind'.[19]

In the absence of memoirs or personal recollections, it is difficult to gauge his spiritual development. An insight, however, can be gleaned from texts he selected from a 1791 Dublin imprint of the Bible to which Edmund Rice subscribed.[20] These twelve texts which he transcribed under the heading 'Texts against Usury' provide the key to his scriptural inspiration:

> But love ye your enemies; do good and lend, hoping for nothing thereby; and your reward shall be great, and you shall be the sons of the Highest; for He is kind to the unthankful, and to the evil [Luke 6:35].

The choice of these texts, one commentator believes, reflects Rice's image of God in that he was attracted by the notion of the covenant between Yahweh and his people. 'This covenant idea for Edmund Rice was a merchant concept: a bargain, a contract, that he could understand'.[21]

On another level, the selection may reflect unhappiness on Rice's part with his business practice to date. Some Catholic merchants had added to their fortune by money lending. While there is no proof that Edmund Rice engaged in the practice, given the recollection that the Rices were 'endowed by a too keen sense of business', it is not improbable that he did.[22] Besides this, there was rumbling controversy amongst the Catholics of Munster throughout the eighteenth-century on the morality of lending at interest. As late as 1824 Bishop Coppinger of Cloyne declared that he was 'fully aware that many worthy ecclesiastics have their scruples upon legal interest'.[23]

Concern for social justice was reflected in his involvement in many of the charitable societies present in Waterford at this time. In the absence of a formal mechanism for state intervention prior to the establishment of poor law schemes in the 1830s, the alleviation of distress was left principally to private charity. Waterford had a number of Catholic charitable societies. In 1771 the Butler and Fitzgerald charities established two hostels each; in 1779 the Wyse charity provided a further three. In 1793 Edmund Rice was among the founding members of the Trinitarian Orphan Society, which maintained the large Congreve mansion on New Street where one hundred boys and girls were housed and educated.[24] In the following year, during a time of particular famine and distress in the city, Edmund was among the founders of the Waterford Society for visiting and relieving distressed room-keepers.[25] Rice had also particular concern for the plight of prisoners, whom he visited and assisted materially. This was to be a constant feature of his life and special apostolate of the early Christian Brothers.

There are two fascinating accounts of individual beneficiaries of Rice's charity. One was a poor black slave boy who Edmund saw on the deck of a vessel at the quay in Waterford. Reflecting sentiments of his contemporary Wilberforce, Rice bought the boy from the ship's master and entrusted him to the care of the Presentation Sisters on Hennessy's Road. When the boy grew he worked as a messenger for the sisters and later Edmund helped him purchase a premises at Gracedieu. In time 'Black Johnnie' succeeded in business and on his death his property, consisting of two houses, was left between the Christian Brothers and the Presentation Sisters.[26]

A second beneficiary was the young Italian immigrant, Charles Bianconi, whom Rice advised and helped secure a premises in Clonmel. In time Bianconi established a thriving transport system and was elected Mayor of Clonmel, but he never forgot his early benefactor and each year sent £50 and twenty suits of clothes for poor boys. His appreciation for the 'good friend who took a kindly interest' in him was reflected in a clause of his will which ran 'failing direct issue, I bequeath to the Christian Brothers the reversion of my property'. Bianconi was survived by a daughter.[27]

IV

The 1790s was a crucial decade in modern Irish history. Under the influence of the French Revolution the country witnessed unprecedented politicisation and an inevitable part of popular agitation was directed towards securing the repeal of the remaining penal laws. After 1778 and 1782, the bulk of the religious and economic disabilities had been removed, but the political restrictions remained on the statute book. Since the middle of the century, Catholic interests had been represented by an ineffectual Catholic Committee. Already by the 1780s, tensions had begun to develop within this body as the confident new middle class began to challenge the old aristocratic leadership. In the past the Committee had been content to beg relief from their 'gracious sovereign' in deferential terms, but under the influence of French ideology this more aggressive faction demanded redress for Catholic grievances as a right rather than a reward to be sought with deference.

Waterford had played a prominent role in Catholic politics of the eighteenth-century; in the 1750s the leadership of the Catholic Committee was largely provided by Thomas Wyse, one of a wealthy mercantile family with continental connections. It was understandable that ambitious, prosperous Catholics with outside interests would turn their attention to political disabilities and Edmund Rice was no exception. In 1792 the Irish parliament passed a relief bill which granted minor concessions to the Catholics. Nevertheless, sufficient concessions were made to turn the debate into an anti-Catholic tirade. The parliamentary session generated considerable resentment within the Catholic community and there was particular bitterness amongst the Catholic Committee at the insults hurled in their direction. The Committee were dismissed in parliament as 'shop-keepers and shop-lifters', 'men of very low and mean parentage'. Wolfe Tone, its secretary, reacted strongly to the depiction of the Committee as a 'rabble of obscure porter-drinking mechaniks' meeting in 'holes and corners'.[28]

These attacks placed the Committee on the defensive, but resentment quickly gave way to anger. In March 1792 it published a Declaration, demonstrating that the principles of Catholicism were in no way incompatible with the duties of citizens or 'repugnant to liberty, whether political, civil or religious'. The declaration answered many of the attacks levelled at Catholics during the parliamentary debates; it renounced all interests in forfeited estates and declared that, if restored to the elective franchise, they would not use the privilege to 'disturb and weaken the establishment of the Protestant religion or Protestant government' in the country.[29] The Committee decided to muster as much support for this Declaration as possible. Chapel meetings were held around the country for this purpose and, together with Bishop Egan and Dean Hearn, Edmund Rice was among one hundred leading Catholics of Waterford to sign the declaration.[30]

The Committee mounted equally forceful campaigns in 1793 and again in 1795, but on these occasions Edmund's name was absent from the Waterford Addresses. Nor does his name appear amongst the Memorial of the Catholics of Waterford in favour of a legislative union in 1799.[31] It would appear that Edmund's mind was turning increasingly from political to religious matters. His brother John returned from Cadiz in 1792 to join the Augustinians at Callan. Edmund himself was contemplating taking a similar course.

The outbreak of rebellion in 1798 however, made it impossible for him to ignore the tragedy around him. His extensive business contacts and military contracts guaranteed his geographic mobility and during the rebellion he was one of the few who were allowed pass unchallenged at all the military posts in Carrick, Waterford, Clonmel, Tipperary and Limerick.[32] In the following year, he witnessed the grisly execution at the jail of Waterford of Francis Hearn, a former student at Carlow College and nephew of Dean Hearn, Rice's friend.[33] Fortunately Edmund Rice was in a position to save from execution the husband of his sister-in-law, Jane Murphy. John Rice of Newlands, county Kilkenny, a colourful character known as 'The Wild Rapparree', had fallen foul of the authorities in 1798. Edmund hid him in his home until an opportunity arose and then he was smuggled in a barrel to Newfoundland.

4

Decision

The death of his young wife in 1789 marked a pivotal point in the spiritual development of Edmund Rice. Working from his brokenness, his priorities changed perceptibly and the alleviation of the misery of others became a primary concern. While initially the desolate merchant considered the classic flight from the world, the chronic poverty of Waterford city convinced him that it was there he belonged, rather than the secluded cloisters of Melleray. Central to the realisation of this was the example of two near contemporaries, Bishop Thomas Hussey of Waterford and Lismore and Nano Nagle, foundress of the Presentation Sisters.

I

The primary concern of the educational clauses of the penal code was to restrict contact between Irish Catholics and potential allies amongst their European co-religionists. But no matter how the laws began, in time the provisions were extended to outlaw Catholic schools. The 1709 amendment to the 'Act to prevent the further growth of popery' (8 Anne, c. 3) decreed that:

> Whatever person of the popish religion shall publicly teach school, or instruct youth in learning in any private house within this realm, or be entertained to instruct youth as usher, or assistant by any Protestant schoolmaster, he shall be esteemed a popish regular clergyman, and prosecuted as such ... and no person, after November 1, 1709, shall be qualified to teach or keep such a school publicly or instruct youth in any private house, or as usher, or assistant to and Protestant schoolmaster, who shall not first ... take the oath of abjuration, under a penalty of £10 for every such offence—a moiety to go to the informer.

There is good evidence that this legislation was enforced, at least in the first half of the eighteenth-century. It was perhaps easier for schoolmasters to avoid prosecution than priests, but there are numerous instances of masters being punished. Corcoran in his study of the penal era lists nineteen indictments against popish schoolmasters brought before the Limerick grand jury alone between 1711 and 1722.[1]

The effect of this and similar legislation was to drive Catholic schooling underground, producing in the process the celebrated 'hedge schools'. Much of has been written about the hedge schools and they have become the subject of great lore. Writing in the 1930s, P.J. Dowling compared eighteenth-century education to 'a kind of guerrilla war' where the teacher, like the priest was frequently on the run.[2] Many accounts are excessively laudatory and others dismiss them as places of squalor: in reality the truth lies somewhere in between. A recent commentator has described them as 'private schools established on teacher initiative and existing as long as they proved financially profitable'.[3] In reality, however, the educational restrictions, like the other provisions of the penal laws, were relaxed outside of times of international crisis and political threat. Catholic teachers were operating outside the law, but after 1730 they were largely left undisturbed. In 1731 a House of Lords committee was appointed under Archbishop Hugh Boulter to enquire into the present state of popery: it reported the existence of some 550 popish schools. Some areas were better served than others: the bishop of Clonfert had one school in every parish, while in Ferns there was no 'Popish schoolmaster' in or near the town of Wexford.[4]

The Charter Schools established in the wake of this report prompted the Catholic clergy to systematise their schooling, lest the children be enticed to these proselytising schools. In 1742 John Kent, recommended the establishment of a fund from which a sum would be paid annually to each bishop for the purpose of Catholic education. This suggestion was taken up by Rome. By the second half of the century, then, there was an effective parish school system over much of the country.[5]

In many cases the mass house served as a school during the week and this strengthened the renewed parish structures. The close links with the parish and is reflected in the priority given to the school in episcopal visitations and the Butler reports of Cashel in the 1750s illustrate the important part played by the schoolmaster in parish life. In most cases masters were required to teach catechism and were reprimanded for failure to do so. When Archbishop Butler visited Fr Patrick Ryan outside Templemore, he wrote 'Fr Ryane is directed to recommend to ye schoolmaster to teach Christian doctrine and instruct ye midwifes concerning baptism'.[6]

In the latter years of the eighteenth-century, the number of schools increased rapidly; by the turn of the century, it is estimated that there were over 7000 hedge-schools accommodating as many as 400,000 pupils.[7] The essential point, in this instance, is that these, like 'The Academy' at

Callan, were pay schools: they had to be or else the master could not survive. As late as 1824, it is estimated that approximately 60 per cent of school age children were not attending school, due to a combination of poverty and lack of schools.[8] It was to this section of society that Edmund Rice turned his attention. Writing in 1826 he summed up his thoughts on the penal restriction of education:

> The poor people of this country want education very badly. Among the many cruel penal laws which were enacted against the Catholics of Ireland since the Reformation, there was one which forbade any Catholic to teach school or even to be a tutor in a private house under pain of transportation for life! His being detected in the act of teaching any one subjected him to this terrible punishment without even the formality of a trial ... It was in force for an entire century, and you will judge, it must have great power in demoralising the people.[9]

II

Similar sentiments on Catholic education were expressed by Thomas Hussey who succeeded to the diocese of Waterford and Lismore in December 1796.[10] Born in county Meath in 1746, Hussey had a distinguished international career as chaplain to the Spanish ambassador in London. This position had placed him at the centre of a bustling social scene in the city and his friends included Dr Johnson, Edmund Burke and many of the leading Whigs. Since 1793, he had played a crucial role in the negotiations leading to the establishment of St Patrick's College, Maynooth, and he was rewarded with the presidency in 1795.[11]

Hussey's episcopate was characteristic of the new confidence enjoyed by the Catholic church. From the outset his administration was in stark contrast to the reserve of the penal era. While his predecessor William Egan was consecrated in secret in his sister's house at Taghmon, county Wexford, in 1771, Hussey's episcopal ordination took place in Francis Street chapel, Dublin on 26 February 1797. The ordaining prelate was Dr John Troy of Dublin and he was assisted by the archbishop of Armagh and Bishops Moylan of Cork, Tehan of Kerry and Delaney of Kildare. In further breach with the past, the occasion was marked by the presence of a military guard of honour.

Hussey was the first Catholic bishop to reside in Waterford since the time of Bishop Comerford, who had died in France in 1652.[12] On arrival in Waterford, the new bishop began a formal visitation of his diocese. His initial observations are contained in a letter to Edmund Burke, written in

May 1797.[13] Hussey devotes considerable attention to a description of the schools of the diocese. Within two months of his arrival, Hussey boasted that he had been able to establish a charity school in the principal towns of the diocese in order 'to instruct the children of the poor, gratis, in reading, writing and accounts'. The bishop was particularly concerned at the proselytising activities of the charity schools of Waterford where 'the clergy of the establishment wanted to have no catechism taught but the Protestant one, and seemed inclined to assimilate them to the Charter schools'. Hussey noted how the Quakers of the city, the most numerous branch of Protestants and 'the most regular and industrious sect', had also opposed the illiberality of the established church and resented their children being instructed from the Anglican catechism.

Hussey followed up this visitation with the publication of a notorious pastoral which sent shock waves throughout Ireland.[14] The pastoral, which dealt with a wide spectrum of diocesan concerns, began with the rhetoric normally associated with the hierarchy, but very suddenly changed its tone:

Bishop Hussey

In these critical and awful times, when opinions seem spreading over this island, of a novel and dangerous tendency—when the remnants of old oppressions and new principles which tend to anarchy, are struggling for victory, and which in collision may produce the ruin of religion—when a moral earthquake shakes all Europe, I felt no small affliction and alarm, upon receiving the command of the Head of the Church to preside over the Catholics of these united dioceses.[15]

Hussey's allusions to the French ideology, the politicisation of the United Irishmen and the impending rebellion were stark, but it was the reference to 'the remnants of old oppression' which raised such reaction. This double-edged approach characterised the pastoral and gave rise to much ambiguity as the bishop continually contrasted the present with the 'forgotten' past.

Hussey publically challenged the proselytising schools and urged his priests to resist their efforts:

Stand firm against all attempts which may be made under various pretexts to withdraw any of your flocks from the belief and practice of the Catholic religion. Remonstrate with any parent who would be so criminal as to expose his offspring to those places of education where his religion, faith or morals are likely to be perverted ... if he will not attend to your remonstrances, refuse him the participation of Christ's Body; if he should continue obstinate, denounce him to the Church in order that, according to Christ's Commandment, he be considered as a heathen and a publican.

The priests of the diocese were urged to make their flocks aware that they were members of 'the Catholic communion', not a 'small sect, limited to that country where that sect itself was formed'. They were members of a great church which had lasted 1700 years, thrived in every part of the world and would 'flourish until time shall be no more'. Consequently 'they should not be ashamed to belong to a religion, which so many kings and princes, so many of the most polished and learned nations of the world glory in professing'.

Understandedly, given the tense political atmosphere of the period, the pastoral met with a barrage of criticism. At least five pamphlets appeared criticising its content and questioning its motives. At very best it was a 'saucy contemptuous challenge—daring us to enter anew ... the rancorous field of controversy'.[16] The conservative firebrand Dr Patrick Duigenan believed that it was 'as seditious a publication as any which has appeared in modern times, provoking the Irish Romanists to insurrection'.

The more moderate Thomas Lewis O'Beirne, the Anglican bishop of Meath, reacted strongly to Hussey's advocacy of segregated education and declared that 'the worst enemies of Ireland could not devise a scheme more effectually calculated to keep this distinction of the King's subjects a distinct people forever, and to maintain eternal enmity and hatred between them and the Protestant body'. He was convinced the bishop intended to erect a spiritual wall to replace the civil barriers which were being dismantled. Dr Troy, the Catholic archbishop of Dublin, criticised the pastoral believing it contained 'too much vinegar .. not sufficiently tempered with oil', while there was surprising opposition also from the poor of Waterford who believed that Hussey's sentiments might jeopardise their chances of employment in Protestant households and businesses.[17]

III

Hussey's pastoral was warmly welcomed by Edmund Rice and it provided the impetus he needed to confirm his choice of vocation. One biographer has spoken of 'the natural kinship between the minds and characters of these two men' which 'helped considerably in bringing to fruition the divinely inspired purpose of Edmund Rice'.[18] Conscious of this, the preacher at the great celebration of his month's mind mass in October 1844 referred to the influence of the 'enlightened and apostolic bishop', who 'in troubled times and at considerable risk ... hesitated not to vindicate the cause of free religious education'.[19]

In 1791, there were ten pay schools in the city of Waterford. Two of these were under Catholic management: one conducted by Fr Ronayne and the other by Mr Waters, whose school was attended by Catholics and non-Catholics alike. In these private schools, the annual fee was six guineas for day pupils and thirty guineas for boarders: such charges automatically excluded the children of the working classes. There were no Erasmus Smith or Diocesan schools and a mere eight Parochial Schools were attended by 235 pupils, paying minimal fees. Free education was provided by three endowed schools and it was against these that Hussey directed his attack. These were: the Charter School at Killotran which had between fifty and sixty students. The Blue Coat School for poor girls had thirty-four pupils in residence and the Bishop Foy School, founded in 1707, catered for seventy-five boys.[20]

Edmund had contemplated joining a religious order on the continent, but it appears he was discouraged by his brother, Fr John Rice OSA, and friend Mary Power, the sister of Fr John Power. Both of these urged him to continue his charitable work in the city: Mary Power dissuaded him by pointing to the plight of the poor in the streets of Waterford; 'there's your

Melleray'.[21] In 1796 Edmund wrote to Pope Pius VI outlining plans to establish a community of teachers in Waterford. The Pope encouraged this proposal, as did his friend James Lanigan, bishop of Ossory.[22] There was no shortage of encouragement for his plans and example was provided by the Presentation Sisters, who became the model for Edmund Rice.

Nano Nagle was a wealthy Cork woman who had been educated in France. During the 1750s, she began to run Catholic free schools for the poor of the city. In 1771, she invited the Ursulines to undertake the running of her five schools, but their rule of enclosure made this impossible. In time, Nano Nagle established a congregation of her own, with the sisters living under simple vows. This was a radical departure from the norm, but solemn vows would have restricted their apostolic freedom. The primary purpose of this new congregation was evangelical work among the poor, in which the schools were but one aspect of a broader plan of missionary activity, visitation of the sick and relief of the poor.[23]

The first Presentation Sisters came to Waterford in 1798. The parish priest of St John's, Fr John Power—a close friend of Edmund Rice—proposed to Hussey that a convent be established in the city. With the bishop's approval, he applied to Cork for a community of nuns, but there were no sisters available. By way of consolation, the Presentation Superior promised that if suitable candidates were available they would be trained in Cork. Two relatives of Fr Power, Ellen Power and his widowed sister-in-law Margaret Power, accepted the challenge.

The two Presentation Sisters opened their school in Waterford in November 1798 and from the beginning the project had the eager support of Edmund Rice and he continued to give the community his financial advice. In 1796, he leased a site for the sisters on Hennessy's Road and the early accounts of the convent are partly in his hand writing. He signed the wills of eleven of the early sisters; he invested their dowries and generally acted as their business manager and agent. As late as 1825, such mundane details as a supply of cocoa appears in his writing in the sister's cash book.[24]

Inspired by their example, Edmund now put ideas of a contemplative life behind him. Dr Hussey's pastoral had fired his enthusiasm for Catholic education and Edmund Rice now embarked on his mission to do for the neglected poor Catholic boys of Waterford what Nano Nagle had done for the girls of Cork.

5

Beginnings

In 1800 Edmund Rice stood alone with only his good intentions. The decision to take this radical option, however, had not been made lightly and Edmund possessed the faith and determination to bring his plans to fruition. 'Providence is our inheritance' became his motto and from humble beginnings in a small thatched school house Edmund took the first steps towards the achievement of a revolution in Irish education.

I

A combination of good fortune and business acumen had made Edmund Rice a considerable fortune. The last quarter of the eighteenth-century had witnessed an economic miracle in the Irish agricultural sector. During the period 1770 to 1880 beef exports to Britain quadrupled, butter doubled and pork increased four-fold. By the end of the century 130,000 pigs were slaughtered annually in Waterford and, with guaranteed navy contracts, this brought as much as £520,000 to the city.[1] Booming demand for agricultural produce, however, increased rents and this in turn created land hunger and the injustices opposed by the Whiteboys.

Edmund Rice benefited greatly from this boom. In 1787 he acquired the Rice holding at Ballykeefe on the death of his father. Seven years later he inherited his uncle's thriving mercantile business in Waterford. The young merchant was thus ideally placed to reap the benefits of the economic miracle. Like so many of his class, Rice had a deep mistrust of the banking system, but the repeal of the penal laws allowed him to invest his rewards in property. A deed of conveyance drawn up in 1815 indicates that Edmund held house property as much as 1500 acres in his own right. These lands, together with the Garter Inn at Callan and ten houses in Waterford, were spread over the counties of Kilkenny, Tipperary and Laois.[2] This property had a capital value of £50,000 and rent alone could earn its owner as much as £5000 each year.

Rice was no Saint Francis. He was not a founder who gave up all to follow Christ, but rather he retained his considerable property and investment, and with these financed his great work.[3] Initially Edmund sold his provisioning business to his friend Thomas Quan, who from 1790 had been part of the confraternity in Waterford. The proceeds from this sale financed the purchase of a three acre site at Ballybricken and part of the £3000 spent on construction of a new school.

In theory, at least, the penal restrictions on Catholic education had been repealed by the time Edmund Rice began his great project. In practice however, there were obstacles to be overcome. Gardiner's Relief Act of 1782 declared Catholic schoolmasters legally free to teach on the condition that they took an oath of allegiance and obtained a licence from the local Protestant ordinary. Hercules Langrishe's Act of 1792 made the latter requirement unnecessary, but the benefits of this concession were removed in 1799 by the imposition of a hefty window tax from which non-licensed schools were not to be exempt. It seems probable that Edmund Rice received a licence for his new school. In many cases application was a mere formality, but attitudes varied. In 1799 Anastasia Tobin foundress of the Ursulines in Thurles was granted a licence. In the same year the Presentation Sisters of Waterford made a successful application to Bishop Marley, but as late as 1814 a licence was refused to Fr Peter Kenney S.J. of Clongowes Wood.[4]

Further restrictions threatened Edmund's project. Since 1782 the endowment of Catholic schools was forbidden by law, while the third clause of the 1791 Relief Act forbade the foundation of any association or society bound by religious or monastic vows. The latter restriction, like so many of its kind, was more than likely a dead letter from its enactment. It may indeed have been included simply to placate the bitter opposition to Catholic relief from the loyalist faction in parliament. The question of endowment was a more serious obstacle, which was further complicated by the 1793 Relief Bill which forbade the establishment of schools and colleges exclusively for Catholic education. In the short term Edmund could afford to ignore these impediments. He had not yet considered religious consecration and the schools would be financed from his own purse. In the long term, however, he would be forced to investigate the penal restrictions of the law, particularly in the wake of O'Connell's 'emancipation' in 1829.

Without waiting for the completion of a permanent school Edmund began teaching in an old stable in New Street. This building, known for many years as 'Elliott's', may have been inherited from his wife—if so, no location could have been more appropriate for his mission to begin. Edmund moved from Arundel Place and now lived above the stable, where below three rooms were fitted out for school. Conditions were primitive: furniture was sparse and benches were borrowed each day from Buggy's pub in Barrack Street.[5] The historian of the Christian Brothers has left us with a, perhaps idealised, description of the master and his first pupils in 1802:

Very soon the rooms were filled with boys, poor lads utterly ignorant of even the first notions of religious or secular knowledge.
They were rude and rough in manner and not all amenable to the
salutary restraints of school discipline. But Edmund Rice, joining
to a commanding presence an agreeable and winning manner, gained
the confidence of the most wayward, and soon established regular-
ity and discipline in the school.[6]

The early days were a learning experience for the teacher as much as his
students. He began on a modest scale—perhaps teaching a group of six
pupils in a night school—but before long the rooms were thronged to the
extent that he was forced to open a second school in Stephen Street
nearby. Gradually Edmund assembled strips of land at Ballybricken where
he intended to build a school. Through the influence of friends in the
Wyse Trustees he was able to acquire the site of the old Faha chapel and,
in a reflection of his close bonds with the Presentation Sisters, he pur-
chased a small passageway leading to their convent on Hennessy's Road
where he could hear mass.

From the beginning Thomas Hussey was an ardent supporter of Edmund
Rice's plan. His pastoral had prompted Rice to take the great step and he
had laid the foundation stone of the new school in June 1802. During that
year, however, a strange coolness developed between the two: the bishop
lost interest in the school and appears to have become quite hostile. The
explanation for this unexpected change is unclear, but it may be attributed
to two factors which surfaced frequently in Edmund Rice's life; jealousy
and the question of episcopal authority.

Jealousy needs no explanation, but the latter proved a thorny issue. A
combination of his own character and fortunate circumstances made Rice's
venture extraordinarily independent and open to resentment and misun-
derstanding. He had supplied both the initiative and the finance and in
this way was answerable to no one, least of all the local bishop. This was
complicated further by the fact that the Faha site had previously been
ecclesiastical property which had been leased to Rice by Dean Hearn
acting for the diocese in the absence of the bishop.[7] Thomas Hussey was
a prickly individual: his service in the Spanish Embassy in London had
made him extremely conscious of protocol and he jealously guarded what
he regarded as the episcopal prerogative. Unwittingly, Edmund Rice had
offended the bishop's sensitivities; he had stepped beyond the acceptable
limit, establishing a Catholic school free from clerical supervision. Fr John
Power, one of his oldest friends, suggested a way out of this delicate
situation. He advised Edmund to draw up a deed of assignment handing
the site over to the bishop, reserving only a life interest for himself. In this
way, Power believed, he would 'prove [his] submission to his Lordship

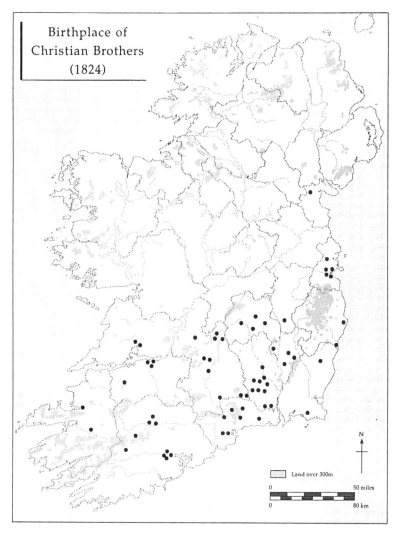

Birthplace of Christian Brothers (1824); courtesy of Kevin Whelan

and the baseless character of the stories he has been told, as well as the vileness of the motives ascribed to [him].[8]

It is perhaps idle to speculate on the nature of 'the stories' and the 'vileness of the motives' attributed to Edmund Rice, but no doubt there were many in the city who remained cynical about Rice's conversion, especially if suspicions of his being engaged in money lending and aggressive property speculation were true. In any event, Bishop Hussey was

content with Edmund's gesture of submission. The deed was duly registered; an important milestone had been passed, Rice had brought his
mission under episcopal supervision, and secured a generous benefactor in
the process.

Thomas Hussey blessed the completed residence at Ballybricken in
June 1803. The story is told that it was he who gave it the name which
would become famous. Commenting on the raised site outside the city,
Hussey alluded to the Holy City; 'all things considered, I think a very
appropriate name would be Mount Sion, and so I name it'.[9] One month
later the bishop died suddenly at Tramore on 11 July, having taken a fit
while swimming there. Even in death Hussey managed to rouse strong
feelings and his funeral became the scene of a violent protest. As the
remains were being brought to Waterford for burial, the procession was
interrupted by a group of drunken soldiers returning from an Orange
meeting who tried to throw his remains into the Suir. Thomas Hearn later
described for Lord Donoughmore how this mob had 'uttered the most
abusive threats to cut up his remains and his friends'.[10] Amongst those
friends was Edmund Rice to whom Thomas Hussey left the greater part
of his estate; apart from a bequest of £2000, each master was to be paid
£20 per annum and Rice was to receive a salary for life.[11]

II

From the outset it was clear that Edmund Rice intended his schools to be
more than just that. Within months of opening his school in New Street
he was joined by two Callan men, Thomas Grosvenor and Patrick Finn,
and together they formed a religious community: they prayed together,
attended daily Mass and devoted time to spiritual reading. Bishop Hussey's
last report to Rome in June 1803 gave a description of their position:

First Profession of Edmund Rice and his companions

some few men have been formed into a society who eagerly desire to bind themselves by the three solemn vows of chastity, poverty and obedience under the rules similar to those of the [Presentation] Sisters, and already a convent has been built where four holy men reside who seek approbation of their rules whenever it will be deemed advisable by the Holy See.[12]

In his will, too, Hussey referred to Edmund Rice not by location but, 'of the Society of the Presentation'.

From the beginning then, Rice and his companions followed the vision which would later be enshrined in the first chapter of the constitutions of his society:

The end of this congregation is that its members labour in the first place for their own perfection, and in the second for that of their neighbour by serious application to the instruction of male children especially the poor, in the principles of religion and Christian piety.[13]

The school at Mount Sion opened its doors and was blessed by Hussey's successor and Rice's old friend, Bishop John Power, on 1 May 1804. Already there were over three hundred boys on the roll and the accommodation proved inadequate. Additional rooms were secured and the brothers opened a night school to educate the illiterate and instruct them in the catechism.

The brothers' charity extended beyond the provision of education. A small bakehouse was built to provide the poorer pupils with a daily meal of bread and milk. For many years, too, a tailor was employed at Mount Sion repairing tattered clothes and distributing suits to the poor. The plight of prisoners remained a priority. Contemporary reports commented that the Brothers were 'ever to be found' administering to prisoners and alleviating their sufferings.[14] Many of the *Memoirs* recall Edmund's visits to the cells and how he often escorted condemned men to the gallows:

This was a special privilege extended to Br Rice as he was credited with having a wonderful power of moving to repentance some of those hardened people who seemed callous when appealed to by the clergy even.[15]

III

By 1810 Edmund Rice had a comprehensive system of education in place. This was applied in each of the schools of his fledgling congregation and in time it became a model which others followed. The fullest description of the regime is contained in a letter written by Rice in reply to a request from Archbishop Bray of Cashel [see Appendix 2]. Every minute of the school day, from nine to three o'clock, was accounted for and this programme reflected an adaptation of several systems for educating large numbers.

A striking feature of the regime was the priority attached to the religious and moral formation of the pupils. Reading was taught from Fr William Gahan's *History of the New and Old Testament*. Comments were made on the text and considerable time was reserved each day for 'general moral instruction' and lessons from the Catechism or Gobinet's *Instruction of Youth in Christian Piety*, first published at Paris in 1665. 'This half-hour explanation of the Catechism', Edmund Rice believed, was 'the most salutary part of the system'. There were set times for prayer; at noon the students recited the Angelus and Acts of Faith, Hope and Charity: at three o'clock the Salve Regina and the Litany of the Blessed Virgin were said, while the day was punctuated with the Hail Mary on the strike of every hour. Children were prepared for the sacraments and the confessions of the entire school were heard at least four times each year.

There were many original ideas in Rice's scheme, including the strict limitation placed on corporal punishment. Pupils were not grouped by age, but 'according to their degrees of improvement'. Each brother had charge of 150 boys and the combined efforts of monitors and masters ensured each boy received personal attention. A further novelty was the existence of a lending library in the school, containing about one hundred and fifty books, which the boys were encouraged to read to their parents at night. Pious books were also supplied to apprentices in the town who were obliged to attend the sacraments once a month. This latter provision reflected the exclusive nature of the system, which included the prohibition of students playing or keeping company with pupils from other schools.

Inevitably, given these emphases, Edmund Rice's system was not without its critics. Few challenged his pedagogical method, but most rounded on the religious ethos of the schools and the perpetuation of 'popish superstition'. The traveller, Henry Inglis' observations were typical of many:

> The most important institution I visited [in Waterford] was a Catholic school at which upwards of 700 children were instructed ... although I am far from questioning the motives of the founder Mr Rice or the young men who thus made a sacrifice of themselves, yet I cannot regard favourably an institution under such tuition. I know too much of Catholicism in other countries to doubt that intellectual training will be made very secondary to theological instruction ... I would rather not see a system of education exten-

sively pursued in which the inculcation of popish tenets forms so chief a part'.[16]

Writing in 1825, one malevolent critic condemned the Brothers' schools as 'the most intolerant and mischievous which any individual or society has attempted to mask under the disguise of Christian instruction':

> Nothing could be more hopeless, in a human sense, than the task of attempting to eradicate the peculiar impressions which are burned into juvenile feeling by the operation of the system. There are about 6,000 orthodox larvae in these poisonous receptacles, and the queen bee, it seems is still in vigorous operation.[17]

Such criticism was understandable, given the heightened sectarian tensions of the 1820s, but there were many Anglicans who were generous in their praise. Dean Ryland of Christ Church believed the schools had brought 'incalculable benefit' to the city, while the liberal member of parliament for Waterford, Sir John Newport, entertained 'the highest possible opinion of the system pursued in Mr Rice's .. school'.[18]

The motto of Edmund Rice remained constant: 'Catholic and Celtic, to God and Ireland true'.[19] The pursuit of this ideal fired him; he was unmoved by praise or criticism and placed all his trust in Providence. If assurance was necessary, however, this was to be found in the the numerous requests for communities received from bishops throughout Ireland and beyond.

Bishop Francis Moylan of Cork

6

Expansion

From the first tentative steps in Elliott's yard Edmund oversaw the rapid progress of his venture. Yet he, least of all, could have anticipated the success of this great mission of charity. From humble beginnings the halls of Mount Sion soon thronged with youth eager to be freed from the want that was their lot. The inspiration of this mission, however, was not mere philanthropy or compassion; Edmund and his companions were moved with a religious zeal and before long others accepted the scriptural injunction to 'come and see'.

I

A great deal has been written about the Gaelic survival of south Leinster and east Munster. Under the sympathetic influence Catholic or crypto-Catholic grandees the region was sheltered from the full rigors of the penal laws. Through a combination of collusion and connivance the Catholic interest was protected an extended. Beneath the sub-gentry there was a layer of strong farmers who had advanced from the small-farm ranks and these developed a complex web of connections with their co-religionists in the towns. Increasingly, this aggressive, articulate, class supplied the leadership of the Catholic community. While the aristocratic influence of the Dillons, O'Conors and Taafes had waned by mid century, the transformation was completed 1791 by the ejection of Lord Kenmare and his associates from the leadership of the Catholic Committee. In their place, direction was provided by Edward Byrne, one of the largest merchants in Dublin—'a sugar-baker, seller of wine and other commodities'—and John Keogh, 'a retailer of poplins in Dame Street'.[1]

The patterns of clerical leadership changed in parallel. The economic restrictions of the penal era favoured the promotion of financially independent-gentry candidates to the episcopacy. By the end of the century however, they were drawn increasingly from the ranks of the middle-class: Thomas Hussey was a farmer's son; Archbishop Troy's people were merchants in Smithfield, while Bishop James Lanigan was the son of a grocer in Carrick.[2] The great religious founders of the late eighteenth and early nineteenth-century came from similar backgrounds. Edmund Rice and

Nano Nagle epitomise this group, whose numbers included the heiress, Catherine McAuley, the Dublin milliner Teresa Mullaly and Frances Ball, the first Loreto sister and daughter of a prosperous Dublin silk merchant.[3] These well-educated, confident founders were highly motivated and many in their close-knit circle were attracted by their values and vision.

Edmund's first disciples were drawn from among the strong farmer and merchant ranks. His earliest followers were Callanmen, Patrick Finn and Thomas Grosvenor. In time they were joined by John Mulcahy, a former clerical student from Cappoquin, John Power, nephew of the bishop of Waterford and Patrick Murphy, uncle of Margaret Aylward, the Foundress of the Holy Faith Sisters. The early group included two wine merchants, John Watson of Dublin and Thomas Brien from Waterford; something of the diversity of the group is reflected in the presence of the convert Benjamin Francis Manifold, who had served in the Wicklow militia, and the Callan cobbler, Thomas Cahill, who had been flogged in for his part in the 1798 rebellion.

In a similar way, Edmund Rice was able to tap the enthusiasm and financial resources of the Catholics of the area, often in a dramatic fashion, as when a merchant personally sponsored a school in his town.[4] This was the case in 1807 when William Barron of Faha left £1000 to erect a school in Dungarvan. With the bishop's approval, John Mulcahy was sent to take charge of the venture which attracted two hundred students on its opening day. Not one of these boys had previously been at school.[5]

Local response was the key element in the diffusion of the early schools. The erection and maintenance of even the most basic school houses required considerable resources and the creation of a system of schools was beyond the limit of Rice's fortune. Along with this, the competition for scarce resources was intense, and chapel building generally took precedence over the provision of schools. In this scenario, the stimulus for education often came, not from the clergy, but from the Catholic upper middle class. Where financial support was available the nuns and the brothers could be invited to open free schools. It is this factor which explains the initial diffusion of the Christian Brothers in the prosperous crescent running from Waterford to Limerick.[6] The circumstances surrounding the establishment of Edmund Rice's second school, at Carrick-on-Suir, illustrates many of these features.

Carrick was a town of extremes. In 1834 the traveller Henry Inglis described it as 'distinguished in nearly equal proportions, by ... exquisite opulence and soft beauty ... and by the haggered misery, the squalid poverty ... which characterises the great body of its population.'[7] Yet despite this poverty, the town experienced the wave of ecclesiastical renewal which characterised the province. A new chapel was built in Carrick in 1804 and two years later the parish priest built a new house for himself.

The new chapel was an ambituous construction; a contemporary has left an account of its dimensions:

> It is 82 feet long by 62 feet wide, making it 5004 square feet, which sat 2 feet to each person will acccommodate 1250 persons, and galleries 17 feet wide and quite round the house will accommodate 94 persons more. The lower floor will hold ... within 94 persons of double the old chapel lower floor will.[8]

The scale of the chapel reflected the increased population of the town, but was perhaps also an indication of more regular Mass attendance. The chapel was financed by general subscription and the surviving list of contributors supports our earlier observations. Once more, it was the mercantile class which promoted and financed this venture, while the vast majority of the population, the labourers, fishermen, factory workers, made no contribution whatever to the fund. This might be attributed to either their poverty or a sense of alienation from the predominantly middle class church.[9]

Similarly the school at Carrick was financed by the contributions of two substantial benefactors. The site for the school was bequeathed by a local man, James Doyle, and the costs involved were borne by public subscription. The monastery, built at a cost of £1500, was financed by a donation made by one of Edmund Rice's friends and first disciples, the wine merchant Thomas O'Brien who was the oldest of the early brothers. The school opened in January 1806 and was attended by sixty 'rude, ignorant and uncultivated' boys.[10] In the same year a free school was opened for girls. From the beginning there were close links between the parish and the brothers. The parish priest, John McKenna, gave encouragement to the venture, visiting the school and celebrating Mass for the 'monks and scholars'. It is perhaps a measure of the efforts of the brothers that eight hundred children were presented for Confirmation in July 1807, apparently the first time the sacrament had been administered in the parish since Dr Hussey's visitation in 1802.[11]

II

From the beginning Edmund and his companions lived the life of religious at Mount Sion. There they gathered in prayer before the Blessed Sacrament and lived according to an adaptation of the Presentation rule. Thomas Hussey had informed Propaganda Fide, in 1803, of the existence of this group of 'holy men', their desire to be bound by the solemn vows and their intention to petition the Holy See for an approved rule.[12]

No moves were made towards a formal recognition of the monks', as the brothers were called, until the summer of 1808. Various reasons have been given for this delay; the penal prohibition on the formation of new religious orders and the question of exclusively Catholic schools and issue of endowments, but none of these explanations are particularly convincing.[13] Similarly, Rice's decision to apply for religious profession in 1808 has been attributed to changing political circumstances which suggested 'the dawn of emancipation was on the horizon'.[14] Neither is this explanation satisfactory; the duke of Portland's administration was not only ready to shelve the emancipation issue, but had fought the 1807 general election successfully on a 'no popery' platform. In these circumstances Grattan's petition for emancipation had little hope of success and the emergence of controversy on the proposed royal veto on episcopal nominations blighted future hopes of success.[15]

The decision to apply for religious profession was more likely due to practical rather than political considerations. It was eight years since Edmund had begun his mission in Elliott's yard; there were now three communities in the fledgling congregation and nine monks were living the life of Christian educators. Within the diocese, too, Edmund enjoyed the support of the clergy and Bishop John Power had been among his closest friends and supporters. All of these factors indicated that the oppurtune moment had arrived.

Bishop Power welcomed Edmund's request for profession and it was agreed that the three communities would assemble at Mount Sion on the feast of the Assumption to make their commitment in common. On that day eight brothers made annual vows according to the rule and constitution of the Presentation Order. One of Edmund's earliest followers, Thomas Brien of the Carrick community, chose not to proceed. Despite his well-intentioned zeal, the rigors of the life had proved too much and, on medical advice, he returned to Waterford where he resumed his business.

The brothers were now religious living in temporary vows under episcopal sanction, but all concerned were anxious that the congregation would be placed on a secure footing. With this in mind, Bishop Power submitted a petition to the Holy See requesting Apostolic approval of the new Institute. This appeal met with a favourable response from Propaganda Fide which granted provisional approval, pending the submission of a rule and constitutions.[16] Encouraged by this development, Bishop Power agreed to admit the brothers to perpetual vows in 1809. Once more, however, it saddened Edmund that not all his companions would make this long hoped for profession. John Power returned home, while Edmund's first disciple, Patrick Finn, left Ireland to join the Cistercians in Melleray. He returned in 1833 and was among the founding members of the community at Mount Melleray, county Waterford.

III

The young congregation lived an austere lifestyle. The brothers rose each morning at five o'clock and spent one hour in prayer and meditation. This was followed by spiritual reading and Mass. After school the spiritual exercises resumed with a visit to the Blessed Sacrament, the Little Office of the Blessed Virgin and further spiritual reading. The day ended with the recital of the Rosary.

The brothers' meals were frugal. Breakfast consisted of porridge with bread, butter and milk; tea was not used until 1829. Dinner was at about 3.30 pm and this was the last meal of the day. Edmund prescribed the Lenten fasts in the Rule and throughout the year there were at least two meatless days per week. In addition the brothers practiced various corporal austerities, including the use of hair shirts, chains and disciplines. In the chapter of 1829 Edmund made an unsuccessful attempt to have included in the Rule a paragraph encouraging the use of hair shirts and other disciplines.[17]

Edmund Rice made great demands on himself. The Annals of the Christian Brothers recall that he was 'a mortified man, he denied himself in a variety of ways, but made no display of the acts of his virtue'.[18] There is, however, one dramatic recollection of his self denial:

> For many years he had been a great snuff-taker. In one of his annual retreats he resolved to give up the habit completely. As if to signalise his renunciation of this luxury, he threw his snuff box into the fire and never after took snuff.[19]

Since his early years in Waterford, Edmund had been acquainted with the Jesuits in the city. In particular he was impressed by the venerable priest Father Barron and it appears that he encouraged Thomas Quan, Peter StLeger and the other members of Edmund's confraternity to make the Spiritual Exercises of St Ignatius annually.[20] This connection with the Jesuits continued throughout Edmund's life and it was their influence which prompted him to take Ignatius as his name in religion.

In spite of this Edmund Rice's spirituality was predominantly Teresian. In his youth he relied on Scupoli's *Spiritual Combat* and *The Imitation of Christ*, but as he matured the major influence on his spiritual development were the writings of St Teresa of Avila. One of his early companions recalled his devotion to the saint:

> He was remarkably devout to St Teresa: her feast day was always one of special devotion to him, and from him all his early companions took up this devotion. He kept a picture of the saint in his room, and often he would be seen pressing his lips to it. His

devotion to the great saint became more remarkable as his life drew to a close, but as might be expected his devotion to the Holy Mother of God was most intense.[21]

Above all, Edmund was renowned for his intense Eucharistic devotion. From the first day at Mount Sion the Brothers had permission to reserve the Blessed Sacrament in their oratory, and apart from the visits prescribed by the Rule, he would visit the oratory before and after school and when leaving or returning to the house. This and other devotions he encouraged in the younger brothers.

IV

Wherever possible, Edmund Rice responded favourably to invitations to open schools. In reply to a request from Archbishop Bray of Cashel in 1810 he expressed a wish that his system would 'spread before long in most parts of the Kingdom'.[22] There were, however, strict limitations which restricted his freedom to meet the many requests which came to him. Apart from the obvious financial considerations, the shortage of manpower was the greatest impediment to renewed expansion. Circumstances necessitated choices; Edmund increasingly devoted his scarce resources to the provision of education in the cities. The early years of the nineteenth-century witnessed a dramatic increase in the population of Ireland; in the thirty years from 1792 numbers rose from four and a half million to almost seven million. Educational needs were more pronounced in the cities where the poor, unable to pay fees, were left uncared for. It was to this section of society that various institutes of religious men and women devoted their attention.

The Brothers were invited to Cork by Francis Moylan, the great patron of Catholic education. Since his appointment in 1787 Bishop Moylan had made every effort to promote the education of the poor; he had facilitated Nano Nagle's request for Apostolic approval of her congregation and in 1793 he was among the founders of the Cork Charitable Society, established to provide free education for boys. By 1808 the Society had eleven schools under its direction catering for the needs of seven hundred students, but this was totally inadequate in a city of 80,000 people. Besides, the inefficiency of the teachers meant that the future of these schools was far from secure.

No member of the Waterford communities could be spared. Just as Waterford had sent the Power ladies to the Presentation Novitiate in 1796, so Edmund Rice accepted two candidates from Cork to Mount Sion in 1809. On Moylan's suggestion, Jeremiah O'Connor and John Leonard, both members of his Charitable Society, travelled to Waterford to begin

their novitiate and subsequently made their solemn profession before returning to Cork. Their first school was a small room in Chapel Lane,
which until 1811 had been conducted by paid teachers. Before long the
brothers had wrought a change in the city. Of this achievement Fr John
England, one of the education Committee, could write in 1815:

> The vast improvements in the system of educating the poor which
> have taken place within the last few years are, even to the Commit-
> tee which has witnessed the gradual progress, matter of surprise
> and consolation.[23]

In that same year Bishop Moylan died and left a substantial bequest to the
Brothers, who he described as 'his successors'.

The foundation of the great North Monastery was laid in 1814. The
monastery was finished and occupied within two years. The school, however, was not opened until 1818, because it was placed at the disposal of
the Committee of Public Health during the typhus epidemic which dev-
astated the city. During this crisis the Monastery served as a hospital and
two of the community, Jerome Ryan and Ignatius McDermott, died caring
for the sick.

Similar circumstances pervailed in Dublin. In the last quarter of the
eighteenth century there were forty-eight Catholic schools in the city and
these had 1300 boys on their rolls. Only eight of these were free schools
and these could accommodate no more than 255 boys.[24] In the early years
of the new century the Presentation Sisters opened a large school for girls
at George's Hill and the distinguished Jesuit, Dr Thomas Betagh, opened
one or two free boys' schools in the city.

In 1812, Dr Daniel Murray, the Coadjutor Archbishop of Dublin,
invited the Christian Brothers to the city. Fortunately Edmund was in a
position to grant this request and a community was established at Hanover
Street, under the direction of his first disciple, Brother Thomas Grosvenor.
With the community Edmund sent a donation of £387 to help the new
foundation. In time this link with Dr Murray would prove of crucial
significance to the development of the Christian Brothers. Education was
the Archbishop's principal priority and he made every effort to consolidate and extend the presence of the new teaching orders in the city.

Here in Hanover Street amongst the poor of the south docks the
Brothers continued the work which had established their reputation in
Munster. Referring to this great work, a Dublin priest speaking fifty years
later could declare:

> All the pious sodalities, societies and all the teachers in the Sunday
> Schools, and even the ranks of the clergy, were mainly fed from the
> Hanover Street School. The holy and practical Catholics of the

parish, and the regular ones at the confessional during the past twenty years, were all educated in their schools.[25]

The Brothers extended their work in Dublin. In 1818 a school was opened in Mill Street, where six hundred boys were taught in four large rooms in the former city residence of the earl of Meath. This school flourished until 1838 when the lease expired. The community then transferred to Francis Street and subsequently to Synge Street which became the most distinguished of the Brothers' schools. In 1820 another school was established in James Street, where two hundred boys were educated under the direction of Brother Francis Manifold, the former major of the Wicklow militia.

In Munster the expansion continued with the opening of a school in Thurles. As early as 1810 Dr Bray had requested a community for his diocese, but due to a shortage of manpower Edmund was unable to meet this request. Then in 1815, two members of an existing lay community of 'monks' in Thurles travelled to Mount Sion to begin their novitiate. Following their profession they returned to establish a school in the town. Limerick, with a population of 45,000, had particularly pressing needs. A contemporary account described the city as 'the very acme of those evils of starvation, disease and putridity'.[26]

Bishop Touhy had unsuccessfully requested a community in 1812, but Edmund agreed to send three brothers to the city four years later. Resources in Limerick were particularly short. The diocese had no potential

Hanover Street School

candidates for the Congregation, nor had the bishop acquired suitable accommodation for the new school. Coupled with this, the initial response to a charity sermon in aid of the venture was extremely. Br Austin Dunphy attributed this disappointing response to the poverty of the city:

> It is now five o'clock. I am after returning from the chapel in which a sermon was preached. Instead of the £135 which was expected, only £42 has been collected. The times are bad; we must make allowances.[27]

So great was the poverty that the brothers were forced to beg from door to door in order to raise the necessary funds to establish their school. On the opening day of their temporary school two hundred boys presented themselves for admission. In time these numbers grew and the level of defections from the nearby nondenominational Lancastrian School forced its closure. As had been the case in Mount Sion, the brothers in Limerick distributed clothes to the poorer students. The usual donations were a coat, boots, a pair of pants or, for the very young boys, a dress. Records were kept of these donations and between January 1817 and February 1838 some 1551 boys were clothed by the brothers.[28]

The real poor of Ireland, very often, were to be found not in Dublin or Cork, but in the slums of England. With the same generous spirit with which he had responded to the poor of Waterford, Edmund Rice sent communities to minister to this Irish diaspora. The first foundation in England was made in the industrial centre of Preston, Lancashire. Edmund travelled to the city and was so impressed by the educational needs there, that inspite of a chronic shortage of manpower and funds, he immediately dispatched a community to England. In 1825 two brothers took charge of 150 boys and their programme was in response to specific instructions from the local clergy. Edmund Rice outlined their task:

> The duties to be performed in Preston ... are as follows viz:
> 1. Three hours school before noon.
> 2. Three hours afternoon.
> 3. Catechism and Religious Instruction twice a week from 6 to 7 o'clock in the evening for those who do not frequent the school.
> 4. Catechism and Religious Instruction twice a week from 8 to 9 o'clock for those employed in the factories.
> 5. Religious Instruction morning and afternoon on Sundays.[29]

Further schools were opened in Manchester and in 1826 the Brothers took over a Catholic school in Soho, London, where the annalist of the Congregation recorded 'no boy in the school had made his first communion between the year 1803 and the arrival of the first brother in 1826'.[30]

Edmund Rice's mission had expanded rapidly during its first years.

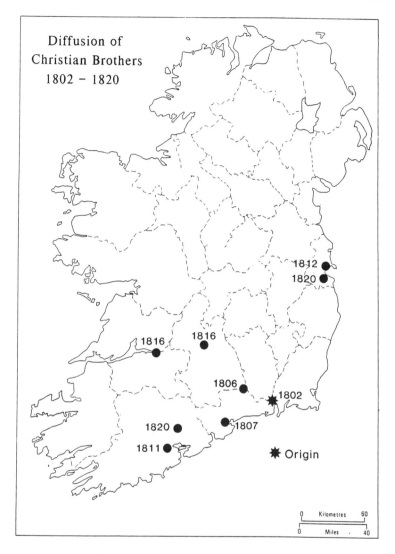

Diffusion of
Christian Brothers
1802 – 1820

1812
1820
1816
1816
1806
1802
1820
1807
1811
★ Origin

0   Kilometres   60
0   Miles   .   40

Diffusion of Christian Brothers Schools, 1802–20; courtesy Kevin Whelan.

The brothers had made an heroic response to the needs of the poor, setting aside the comforts of the middle class to educate the poorest sections of the community. Everywhere their schools had been established the welfare of the poor improved beyond imagination. The life of the Church, too, was greatly renewed by the participation of the previously alienated under-class which the brothers introduced to the renewed discipline and devotion which characterised nineteenth-century Catholicism.

7

Strife

The nineteenth-century was born from the bitter ruins of the 1798 rebellion, yet for the first decades of the century a remarkable degree of tolerance existed between the various denominations on the island. The mass politics of the O'Connellite campaign however, and the efforts of the proselytising societies combined to shatter this harmony and heighten religious tensions.[1] The 1820s was an exciting decade for Irish Catholics which culminated in the Emancipation victory of 1829. Yet these were acrimonious years for both Ireland and Edmund Rice's congregation.

I

The excesses of the 1798 rebellion inevitably revived sectarian tensions. In the aftermath of the rebellion a concerted effort was made to represent the bloody events of that summer as a 'popish plot'. Yet despite the efforts of Richard Musgrave and loyalist historians to revive sectarian memories of 1641 and other atrocities, a surprising degree of religious toleration and co-operation characterised the first decades of the nineteenth-century.[2] There were many manifestations of this spirit. In a celebrated pastoral of 1822, James Warren Doyle ('J.K.L.'), bishop of Kildare and Leighlin, reminded his flock that the Orangemen were their brethren in Christ. A few years later the Catholic bishop and clergy of Limerick walked in the funeral procession of the Protestant vicar general of the diocese. When William Crolly was appointed to the bishopric of Down and Connor in 1825 he entertained a group of about two hundred men to dinner in Belfast an reporter who was present calculated that the majority of those present were Protestant. During this meal toasts were drunk to Bishop Richard Mant and the Protestant clergy of Down and Antrim, the Synod of Ulster and the Presbyterians of Antrim.[3] This same spirit found practical expression in the co-operation in various charitable ventures, such as the Association for the Suppression of Mendicity, established in Waterford in 1821, where Rice served on a predominantly Protestant board.

As the 1820s progressed, however, the practice of ecumenism was becoming more and more difficult. Seán Connolly has attributed this increased sectarianism to three factors: the launch of the so-called 'Second

Reformation', the more combative outlook of the Catholic Church and the emergence of a new style of popular politics.[4] The combination of these factors destroyed the spirit of toleration and resulted in a transformation of the Catholic mind which has become synonymous with Archbishop Paul Cullen of Dublin, who boasted he had never dined with a Protestant. Writing from Rome in 1841, the future cardinal rebuked the 'Apostle of Temperance', Fr Theobald Mathew, for his misguided sentiments:

> I forgot to mention a little matter which I heard some time ago ... It is that in some of the sermons preached by you or attributed to you in the public papers, you appear to entertain sentiments too liberal towards Protestants in matter of religion. I suppose there is no real foundation for this complaint except in the reports of the newspapers which are generally incorrect. However, it is well to be cautious. We should entertain most expansive sentiments of charity towards Protestants but at the same time we should let them know there is but one true Church and that they are strayed sheep from the one fold. We should let them know this; otherwise we might lull them into a false sense of security in their errors and by doing so we would really violate charity.[5]

II

The religious revival which characterised the early years of the nineteenth-century was not confined to the Catholic Church, nor was it simply an Irish phenomenon. This was part of a wider renewal which had swept Great Britain and Ireland, dramatically transforming the religious landscape in process. In Britain one consequence of the so-called 'Second Reformation' was a renewed interest in missionary activity and the Catholics of Ireland were as attractive a target for evangelisation as the heathens of Africa or India.[6] With this task in mind a plethora of missionary societies were formed in Ireland, the more important of which included the Hibernian Bible Society (1806), the Irish Society for Promoting the Education of the Native Irish through the Medium of their own Language (Irish Society) (1818) and the Scripture Readers' Society (1822).

These societies embarked on a vigorous campaign to convert the Irish. Preachers were dispatched to Ireland laden down with Bibles and tracts which they distributed to the poor. Many of these early missionaries were fluent Irish speakers and regarded this skill as a crucial part of their armoury. The distinguished Ulster Methodist, Adam Clarke, declared; 'the Irish language is with the natives a sacred language ... they allow themselves to feel from that tongue, what they do not consider themselves obliged to feel from another'.[7] The British and Foreign Bible Society, which supplied these missionaries, considered making an Irish translation of the Bible, but were initially advised against the move on the grounds that the few Irish peasants who could read, read in English. In time, particularly after the formation of the Irish Society, they were persuaded of the value of such a translation.

The Methodists were among the first to enter the great crusade. John Wesley made his first of twenty-one visits to Ireland in 1747. By 1809 there were twelve Methodist missionaries working in six areas, while ten years later twenty one missionaries worked in fourteen stations dotted around the country. The events of 1798 had convinced Methodists that Catholics were disloyal and violent by nature. One of their missionaries, George Taylor, who had been held captive by the rebels at Gorey, published a history of the rebellion in 1800. This account, depicting the rebellion as a religious campaign, was subsequently serialised in the *Methodist Magazine* . At one point, Taylor comments that 'none of the rebels were so blood-thirsty, as those who were most regular attendants at the popish ordinances'.[8]

The Methodists, like many of the other missionaries, believed their task in Ireland was not simply one of conversion. This was an opportunity to civilise Ireland, to bring the gospel to the deluded Irish peasantry and in so doing, the problems of the island could be solved. More than this, the Methodists looked upon Ireland as the centre of a world-wide conflict between heretical Catholicism and biblical Protestantism.[9]

The historian of Irish Methodism, David Hempton, in his penetrating analysis of this campaign, comments that 'for some peculiar reason Wesley and his followers have been treated with ecumenical kid gloves by a spectrum of twentieth-century writers'.[10] Little of this spirit of tolerance, however, could be found amongst contemporary Catholic commentators who universally identified Methodism with intolerance and opposition. Writing in 1886, the Jesuit, W.J. Amherst reflected these sentiments:

> The Wesleyan Methodists have always been amongst the most bitter enemies of the church. Their founder was not only an enthusiast, but a firebrand. One of his first principles was, no toleration to Catholics; he inculcated it in his followers, and he urged it by actual persecution.[11]

Such bitterness destroyed the liberal spirit of co-operation which had existed between the churches. Rivalry and conflict increasingly became the norm as resurgent Catholicism clashed headlong with evangelical Protestantism. In Cavan one meeting was told that 'Popery and slavery [were] twin sisters', while in Limerick, Bishop Touhy felt it necessary to condemn publicly the calumny directed against the priesthood which had 'become the fashion ... even from the Christian pulpits of our Dissenting brethren.[12] The Catholic clergy, however, were not above such behaviour. Fr Burke of Rosscarbery, Co. Cork, compared English rulers unfavourably with the pagan Romans, while Fr Hayes in Cork allegedly condemned reformers such as Wycliff, Luther and Zwingly, by accusing them of intercourse with the devil.[13]

A great deal of religious rivalry was centred on the education question. Since their first arrival, the provision of schools had formed a vital part of the evangelical crusade. The Bible societies established schools in which free education was offered to all those who were prepared to accept religious instruction. With financial assistance from the Treasury, these bodies set up free schools in places which had previously lacked educational facilities and very often they attracted pupils away from nearby pay schools. The Societies appear to have been most active in poorer counties, such as Cavan or Mayo, where the Catholic revival had not been so pronounced.[14] This trend was particularly evident in Co. Clare where the London Hibernian Society had over eighty schools with one thousand Catholic children on their rolls. According to Bishop O'Shaughnessy these Bible schools had been: 'The cause of diminishing considerably the mutual harmony and friendship between Catholics and Protestants that had subsisted till the unfortunate period of their existence'.[15] Similar concern was expressed by the bishops of Tuam, Ardfert and Galway.[16]

In these circumstances the Christian Brothers were frequently called on to defend the interests of Catholic community against militant Protestantism. Many of Edmund Rice's biographers have focused on this aspect of his career, but from a late twentieth-century perspective it can be difficult to appreciate the great cause of concern.[17] The urgency of the issue, however, is clearly illustrated in the case of Ennis, Co. Clare, where, in 1826, the Bishop made a series of requests to Edmund Rice for a community of 'monks':

> My Dear Sir,
> I am requested by the very Rev. Dean O'Shaughnessy, P.P. of Ennis, to solicit at your hands as a most particular favour, in which I join myself, that you may have the goodness to send to the town ... two competent men of your Brethren, qualified for Religious and literary instruction. There is no town in all Ireland where two Gentlemen of this description could be of more utility, in every point of view ... I beg to hear from you by return of post and hope your answer will be as such as I anxiously wish it. The sooner they may with convenience arrive the better.[18]

By December preparations in Ennis were well under way to welcome the Brothers to the town. In that month the parish priest, Dean Shaughnessy, addressed two letters to Edmund which again reflects both the sense of urgency and the immense respect and deference shown to Br Rice:

> 26 December 1826.
> ... I shall expect them in the first week of the New Year, lest the Biblicals who are endeavouring to make another effort may be in the field before me.
>
> Nothing will be left undone to make the place agreeable to whoever you send & both laity and clergy will feel ever grateful for your condescension in accommodating this town in preference to so many others equally anxious & entitled to your attention.[19]

And again, 16 January 1827: 'The Biblicals are alarmed and fast at work but all to no purpose'.[20]

The Brothers were particularly effective in the cities and there the innovative system of education developed by Edmund Rice was applied with very satisfactory results. These big schools run by the Brothers were in enrolment the equivalent to ten or twelve smaller schools. In Archbishop Murray's Dublin parish there were no fewer than thirty-six Protestant free schools attended by upwards of 1000 Catholic children. To counteract these, Rice opened a temporary school in Jervis Street in 1828.[21]

In Waterford the presence of the 'monks' hampered the work of the missionaries, but attempts were made by the London Hibernian Society to establish a school. In 1824, two members of the Society, Captain George Gordon and Rev. Mr Noel, called a meeting in the City Hall with a view to establishing a school. A large gathering of Catholics and Protestants assembled and when the two gentlemen had finished their address, a local curate, Fr Sheehan, replied from the floor:

> Catholics were charged with being benighted and ignorant but we disprove the assertion, if desired, by sending for any three or four of the humble children educated in Mr Rice's extensive school, and he would fearlessly assert that any one of them would be found as fully informed of the nature of his duties towards God, his neighbour and himself as even the Hon. Gentlemen.[22]

This challenge was not accepted, nor was there a Hibernian School founded in the city. Later that year a meeting of the Catholics of Waterford was held in the Great Chapel to protest against the efforts of the London Hibernian Society. At the end of the meeting a committee was formed to present a petition parliament, calling for full emancipation and denying the malicious allegations made against Catholic schools. Among the members elected to this committee was Edmund Rice.

III

In the face of such staunch opposition, the proselytisers characterised the Christian Brothers as a 'fraternity ... as exclusive and mischievous as it is well possible to conceive'.[23] For these very reasons, however, the Irish bishops were convinced on the great utility of the Brothers in the battle against militant Protestantism. From the outset Edmund Rice had made every effort to respond favourably to the needs of the Church in the various parts of Ireland. Accordingly the spread of his infant congregation had been in response to invitations rather than part of a grand plan, but this had serious consequences which limited its effectiveness.

From their first profession the Brothers had been a diocesan congregation. Each community of the Institute, though united by a common founder and vision, was an independent foundation subject only to the bishop of the diocese. In reality, the local superiors looked to Edmund Rice for guidance and financial assistance, but apart from that the society was a lose body with no official head. In time the weaknesses of this system became apparent.

On one level, the financial needs of the various houses illustrated the desirability of a common fund where scarce resources could be pooled. More fundamental, however, were the restrictions the diocesan structures placed on the Brothers' freedom of response to the needs of the Church. This limitation had been clearly demonstrated following Bishop Murray's request for Brothers for Dublin and the understandable reluctance of Dr Power to release any Brothers from under his control in Waterford.

The Dominican Archbishop of Dublin, John Troy, appreciated the advantages which could be gained from the amalgamation of the various communities under a superior general. His coadjutor, Daniel Murray, was long attached to the idea of centralisation and he, too, urged Edmund Rice to apply to Rome for approval of a Rule and constitutions which would enable him to transfer men from diocese to diocese. Apart from these practical considerations, politically the decision to subject the Brothers to the Holy See alone was of great political significance.

Since the last quarter of the eighteenth-century attempts had been made to subject episcopal appointments to a Royal veto; prior to 1829, it appeared that full Emancipation would only be conceded in return for this safeguard. Edmund had long expressed his violent opposition to such a measure, which he believed would bring 'schism, and every other mischief', and in these circumstances freedom from episcopal control was eminently desirable.[24]

Archbishop Murray suggested that Edmund's companions adopt the Rule of the De La Salle Brothers. On returning from Rome in 1817, Dr Murray brought with him copies of the Rule and Papal Brief of Approba-

Archbishop John Troy

tion of the Institute of the Christian Schools, founded in France in 1680. These provided a model of the kind of central government the new institute needed and they were unanimously accepted by the superiors assembled in Mount Sion in August 1817. These adapted constitutions were transmitted to Rome for approval, along with a memorial from the Brothers and letters from Dr Murray, and Archbishop Troy who was generous in his praise of the Brothers:

> I certify that the Society of laics who supplicate the Holy See for approbation of their Institute, by means of their labours in promoting religion and the moral education of poor boys have done the greatest good for Religion not only in Dublin but also in other parts of this Kingdom. Furthermore I testify that the aforesaid rules of this Society are adapted to the conditions of this country and very suitable for the propagation of the Institute. The testimony of other Bishops in Ireland agrees with me in this matter.[25]

In spite of Archbishop Troy's confidence, the bishops were far from united in their enthusiasm for the proposed amalgamation. The untimely deaths of Bishop Power of Waterford (1816) and Dr Moylan in of Cork (1815) not only deprived Edmund of his closest supporters, but their successors led the opposition to the amalgamation.

The new bishops were disturbed at the prospect of the Brothers being removed from their jurisdiction by the formation of a Pontifical Institute. The fiercest opposition to the amalgamation came from Bishop Robert Walsh of Waterford. Walsh had succeeded to the diocese following a bitter interregnum and he apparently attributed a great deal of the resistance to his candidacy to the influence of Edmund Rice. Along with this, the bishop disagreed with the terms of his predecessor's will. Edmund Rice was Dr Power's executor and as such he opposed Walsh's attempts to have the late bishop's estate, two-thirds of which was bequeathed for the education of the poor, diverted for the upkeep of St John's College.

Accordingly, his opposition to the proposed amalgamation was as much personal as principled and his campaign against the measure degenerated into an assault on Rice's character. In July 1818 he directed a frantic address to Propaganda Fide opposing the plan:

> Indeed most of the Bishops of Munster have written to me deprecating the conduct of some of the Monks, & protesting loudly against the idea of having a perpetual chief or General among them ... My object is, & it is necessary, whereas they are thus unruly & not disposed to live subject to pastoral & clerical superiors, & in order to enforce regularity & order amongst them if they absent themselves about the country for Days without leave either of the Bishop or their respective Pastors, to order that they do not receive the Sacraments—without adhering to their original Discipline nothing can go on well—this unruly, foolish & insubordinate conduct may yet bring the eye of our Protestant Government on them, whom even the Laws as yet do not recognise as a Body & this would be dangerous to us all.[26]

The bishop's letter was followed by similar objections contained in a letter, purporting to come from 'Six Monks' of the Congregation, which opposed Edmund Rice as 'unfit and not capable' of filling the position of Superior General. This letter, a blatant forgery, was filled with inaccuracies, as well as the inclusion of Clonmel (founded 1847), and Youghal (founded 1857) amongst the houses of the order.[27]

A third letter was addressed to the Sacred Congregation in September 1818. This slanderous epistle, which bore the names of seventeen pastors of the diocese of Waterford and Lismore, contained a vicious attack on Edmund Rice:

It may not be amiss to give Your Eminence a brief outline of Rice
the Monk's life ... This man sometimes was a Dealer in cattle and
a common Butcher in the streets of Waterford—Your Eminence
will judge from this, his Slaughtering profession of the savageness
of his nature and absence of tender sensibility and want of human
feeling. This impertinent intruder in the affairs of the sanctuary
was of habits irregular and of desires lustful, which to the prejudice
of morality and the scandal of the faithful he fully gratified—from
his loins issued many a bastard child, some of which breed and
spurious progeny are still living; reflecting on his unprincipled (*sic*)
conduct—this is a truth we all know and so do the laity of Waterford ... —ashamed of his misfortunes, he entered on a religious
life, and how happy the change if he be truly repented and did not
meddle in other people's concerns. Not still satisfied, this wretched
man's ambition also is to become perpetual General of his institute
and to lord it over the Priests and Bishops and be under no controul
(*sic*).[28]

This letter, like the one from the 'six monks', was an obvious forgery
and recognised as such by Propaganda Fide; modern analysis suggests it
was written by the bishop's close collaborator, Patrick O'Meagher, parish
priest of Dungarvan.[29]

Notwithstanding this, Rice's application for approval had to go through
definite procedures. As part of this process Cardinal Fontana requested
further clarification of Troy's testimony of the support of the hierarchy. In
response to this request, the Archbishop effectively marshalled the bishops and, apart from minor reservations, secured the support of sixteen
prelates for the proposed amalgamation. The Brothers were fortunate, too,
in having Fr John Rice in Rome to handle their affairs. By now Edmund's
brother was Assistant General of the Augustinians and he exerted considerable influence through his friendship with Dom Mauro Capellari, the
future Gregory XVI, who was consultor to several Pontifical Congregations.[30]

The decisive factor, however, in securing Papal Approbation was
Edmund's known hostility to the proselytising schools. Cardinal Fontana
had addressed a letter to the Irish bishops in September 1818 in which he
outlined Papal opposition to these schools:

Information has reached the ears of the Sacred Congregation that
Bible Schools, supported by the funds of Catholics, have been
established in almost every part of Ireland, in which, under the
pretence of charity, the inexperienced of both sexes, but particularly peasants and the poor, are allured by the blandishments, and

even gifts of the masters, and infected with the fatal poison of depraved doctrines.[31]

Fontana urged the hierarchy to establish Catholic schools which would defeat this menace and in these circumstances Pope Pius VII must have regarded Edmund Rice's application as an answer to prayer.

It was these considerations which assured the Papal Approbation within an unusually short period of two years. Dr Murray wrote to Edmund Rice, in October 1820, informing him that the Pope had granted the Brief, entitled *Ad Pastoralis Dignitatis Fastigum*. In the same letter the Archbishop prayed that God would 'grant stability to an Institute that promises so fairly to be of essential benefit to the interests of religion in this country'.[32]

IV

Edmund called the Brothers in perpetual vows to a meeting in Thurles on 25 August 1821. Apart from minor reservations there was general acceptance of the provisions of the Brief and it was arranged that those eligible would gather at Mount Sion early in the following year to make their profession according to the new Constitutions. No member of the Cork community attended the meeting at Thurles, nor did they join the new congregation in 1822, in deference to their bishop's wishes. The foundation at Cork in 1811 had been made on Bishop Moylan's initiative and the first brothers had been members of his education committee. As a result of these circumstances the Bishop Murphy of Cork looked upon the North Monastery as his own foundation and tried to preserve his jurisdiction over the brothers. The absence of these brothers from the new Congregation was a source of great sadness to Br Rice.

Nineteen assembled at Mount Sion on 11 January 1822. That evening they began their eight-day profession retreat which was conducted by Fr Peter Kenney, rector of the Irish Jesuits and long time friend of Edmund Rice. On the Feast of the Holy Name, 20 January, the 'monks' made their vows as Christian Brothers. Later that day the superiors gathered in the oratory to form the first General Chapter and they elected Edmund Rice as their Superior General. This body began the patient work of adapting the rules of the Jesuits, the De La Salles and the Presentation Sisters to meet the needs of their own circumstances. After careful deliberation, the rule of the Christian Brothers was printed in 1832.[33]

The Brothers at the North Monastery continued under the jurisdiction of Bishop Murphy. Their circumstances became increasingly difficult and they found themselves at odds with the bishop. One by one they slipped away to Waterford where they made their vows according to the new constitutions. The final crisis occurred in 1826 when Dr Murphy requested the Brothers to make over their property to him by a deed of assignment. The superior refused to meet these demands and he placed the community under the jurisdiction of Edmund Rice and the protection of the Papal Brief. By the summer of 1826 Augustine Riordan was the only brother in the North Monastery who had not joined the new congregation.

Bishop Murphy visited the community in the autumn of 1826 in an attempt to heal differences. The *Presentation Record* (1918) gives an account of this meeting:

> He asked them if they had any complaint to make of his treatment of them ... They replied they had none, but on the contrary expressed sincere gratitude for his fatherly care of them. They then said that it was the interests of the Institute, and through it the interests of the Church in Ireland that induced them to take the step they had determined on. Then the bishop turned to Michael A. Riordan and another who were very dear friends of his, he appealed to them to remain under his jurisdiction ... The two severed their connection with the Brothers of the North Monastery to the very great regret of the Community.[34]

The brothers under the leadership of Br Augustine Riordan remained a diocesan congregation under the jurisdiction of Dr Murphy and continued to live according to the old Presentation rule. The bishop provided them with a house on the south side of the city and this foundation, known as the South Monastery, became the home of the Presentation Brothers. Although the physical link was severed in 1826 the Brothers continued to live out the spirit of their founder Edmund Rice.

Receipt of the Apostolic Brief gave the new Congregation stability and permanence. Apart from the unnecessary, and potentially disastrous, clause which bound the Institute to the provision of strictly gratuitous education, the terms of the Brief enabled the Brothers to extend the scope of their mission. More importantly, Edmund Rice was at the helm once more as all his vision and determination would be needed for the struggles of the next decade.

8

Emancipation?

The recognition of the Christian Brothers as a Pontifical Institute in 1820 marks a milestone in the history of the Irish Church. The Decree of Pius VII was the first formal approval by the Holy See of a religious Lay-Institute of men in Ireland. The timing of this approval is significant in so far as it reflected the vitality of the Church. More than that however, when placed within in the context of the Second Reformation it reflects the renewed confidence and combative nature of Irish Catholicism. These traits were displayed in the political campaign of the 1820s and in the educational battle of the following decades. In both of these campaigns militant Catholicism was triumphant, but these victories were not achieved without significant cost to Edmund Rice and the Christian Brothers.

I

Shortly after the Chapter of 1822 Edmund Rice undertook his first General Visitation of the houses which made up the Congregation. Immediately, it became clear that increased centralisation was necessary if the problems of the various foundations were to be overcome. Central to Edmund's planned renewal of the Institute was the establishment of a new generalate in Dublin. Psychologically Mount Sion had enormous significance for the Congregation: it was there Edmund and his companions had begun their mission and it was there, too, the first group of Brothers had made their religious profession.

Nevertheless, as a generalate Mount Sion had its limitations. The Brothers had enjoyed excellent relations with Bishops Hussey and Power, but their successors Walsh and Kelly were less than supportive of the infant Congregation. In Dublin the Brothers would be assured of the support of their greatest benefactor Daniel Murray and the establishment of a curia there would facilitate the administration of the order. Besides, prior to the amalgamation of the houses, each foundation had admitted and trained its own candidates. It was now Edmund's hope to establish a single novitiate and model school in connection with the new generalate which would give the order a recognisable focus.

Brother Rice met with the archbishop in July 1826 and outlined his plans for a new centre in Dublin. Murray was charmed by this proposal and invited the Brothers to his own parish of St Mary's which had particularly pressing needs. Of the 3000 Catholic children in the parish, 2000 received no education whatsoever, while the remaining one third attended Protestant schools.¹ The Catholic school in Liffey Street was totally inadequate and, on Murray's invitation, a meeting of the combined parishes of the area had established an Education Committee which hoped to fund Rice's new venture. Bryan Bolger, an architect in Dublin Corporation, was commissioned to secure a suitable site, but in the mean time, the Committee acquired a premises in Jervis Street where the Brothers began their school in June 1827. As in the other locations, the three brothers did not restrict their activities to teaching school; they embarked on a wide range of apostolates visiting the near by hospital and instructing the Sisters of Charity in Gardiner Street in the skills of teaching large numbers.

II

Politically too, these were exciting times. The campaign towards Emancipation gained a new momentum in February 1823 with the formation of the Catholic Association. This was an ambitious move in which Daniel O'Connell and Richard Lalor Shiel, leaders of rival factions during the veto controversy, joined together to achieve not simply Emancipation, but a solution to all Catholic grievances.² The new movement had enormous potential. At issue was not merely a proposal to present another petition to parliament in favour of emancipation, but, along with other complaints, the new association opposed tithes, bias in the judiciary and the alleged proselytism of the Kildare Place Society.

In spite of its appeal, however, the association made little popular impact and its survival appeared in doubt until January 1824 when O'Connell proposed the collection of what became known as the 'Catholic rent'. Previously membership of the association was one guinea a year, but O'Connell proposed a new category of members, associates who would contribute as little as a penny per month. Apart from the financial considerations of such a move, the associates would have an investment in the campaign and the masses could be marshalled behind the banner of emancipation. This suggestion met with phenomenal success; by March 1825 the Catholic rent had brought in £16,836, while over the period 1824 to 1829 this rose to over £51,000.³

The participation of the Catholic clergy formed a vital element in the renewed campaign. From the beginning, the Constitution of the Catholic Association had included the clergy as *ex officio* members, and O'Connell made brave promises to the clergy when he announced the 'Catholic rent'. £5000 would be set aside for the education of priests, £5000 was earmarked for building of chapels and presbyteries, while a further £5000 was provided for the use of Catholic schools and the purchase of books. The possibility of a united clerical response to these overtures was now greater than ever: the divisive veto question was in the past and O'Connell's deferential manifesto achieved the desired response. As Bartlett has put it, 'by binding priest to people in a political/religious agitation, the Catholic rent could be seen as a shield against proselytism.'[4]

The clergy threw their weight behind the 'Catholic rent' and the campaign for emancipation in 1824–9; as one Methodist critic remarked, 'the Roman Catholic peasantry was not only deluded by the priesthood, but was now paying a penny a month for the privilege'.[5] Priests acted as agents for the association, organised local committees, addressed meetings, canvassed voters and headed processions to the polling booths. In 1828 one election banner announced that a vote for O'Connell was a 'Vote for Your Religion'.

Eighteen twenty-eight, the year which marked the culmination of the emancipation campaign, began with an enormous show of Catholic solidarity. O'Connell opened the year with 'simultaneous meetings' throughout the country; on 13 January rallies took place in 1600 of 2500 parishes in Ireland as a challenge to the government. As the campaign continued to gain momentum, Catholic confidence was running high. In the spring of

Daniel O'Connell at the bar of the House of Commons

that year Edmund Rice acquired a suitable site for his school at North Richmond Street. Initially he intended the archbishop of Dublin to lay the foundation stone, but Murray suggested that O'Connell should perform the honours.

The Liberator was more than enthusiastic about the prospect; it provided him with an opportunity to restate his interest in Catholic education, while at the same time, the occasion could be turned into a display of strength. Following his discussion with Rice, O'Connell outlined the plans for Richmond Street to the Catholic Association. Apparently they had intended building a model training school, but O'Connell suggested that this could be built in connection with the Brothers. Accordingly the association voted £1500 towards the costs of the Richmond Street school and agreed that the laying of the foundation stone would be made as imposing as possible.

The event became one more of O'Connell's monster meetings and 100,000 joined in the great occasion. A procession of the principal clergy and laity marched from the Corn Exchange to the North Circular Road, where O'Connell addressed the crowd. There he outlined his hopes for the school, delivering a bitter assault to the 'Biblicals' in the process. This was a school founded on 'liberal and not sectarian principles'; 'in this national seminary ... no means would be adopted to proselytise the Protestant child, he would be educated and taught with as much anxiety as the Catholic, but with his religion there would be no intermeddling'.[6] O'Connell concluded his address with praise for 'his dear and old friend, Br Edmund Ignatius Rice—the Patriarch of the Monks of the West'.[7] As one commentator has observed, 'when it became necessary to connect the two worlds of high and popular politics ... O'Connell and his colleagues were fully prepared to do so, with a rhetoric that explicitly linked religious, political and economic grievances'.[8]

Years later, in 1844, when O'Connell was in Richmond Jail he recalled that great occasion for Brother Austin Grace:

> When that stone was laid, I had to stand on it and make a speech. What I said then I now repeat, namely that I expect much from that school and the teaching of your brotherhood ... Education to be suited to this country must be Catholic and Irish in its tone, having for its motto 'Faith and Fatherland'. All engaged in the education of the young should remember that 'As the twig is bent, so the tree inclines'.[9]

Two weeks after that great occasion in 1828 O'Connell announced his candidacy in the Clare election, which he subsequently won by 2057 to 982 votes.

Not all of the Brothers, however, were enamoured by O'Connell's style of politics nor the empty promises made to the Richmond Street school. In November 1828, Br Joseph Leonard, a future assistant general, complained that there was now no hope of getting the grant promised by the Catholic Association. The 'Catholic rent' he dismissed as a campaign 'calculated to support the ambition, of perhaps a single man' and he pointed to the existence of every 'trick, chicane and a monopoly of power' in the association.[10]

In spite of the initial enthusiasm and promises, the Brothers experienced many difficulties in establishing their school at Richmond Street. The principal concern was financial. In the early months funds flowed in, but then dwindled and by 1829 work on the site had ceased. Serious measures were called for: Br Rice approached the archbishop with a view to establishing a general appeal in Dublin. This was done and Dr Murray headed the list of subscribers with a donation of £20. It was also agreed that Br Francis Thornton, superior of Limerick, would tour England in search of funding. This was a successful mission raising £500 which, together with £1000 loaned by Bryan Bolger, was enough to complete the last phase of the building. Edmund Rice's substantial fortune had long been exhausted. He was now in debt, but continued to trust in Providence, a faith reflected in the fact that between October 1828 and May 1832 he had 2773 Masses offered for the success of the Dublin project.[11]

The erection of the building was not the end of the Brothers' difficulties. One problem remained to be resolved: the provision of an adequate water supply. It was customary for Dublin Corporation to provide the service free to charitable institutions, but not alone was Rice's application to the Water Pipe Committee refused, but exorbitant fees were demanded for water facilities. After all their trials the Brothers were not to be deterred by this difficulty: a water diviner was employed and an adequate supply was discovered beneath the site. With everything in place, Edmund Rice, his two Assistants and the Novice Master took up residence in North Richmond Street on 23 June 1831. Two weeks later the new school opened its doors to upwards of six hundred students, almost five years after the Brothers had first discussed the project with Archbishop Murray in 1826.

III

The long awaited Emancipation Bill passed both houses of parliament with comfortable majorities in April 1829. Catholics now enjoyed the right to sit in parliament, be members of any corporation or hold higher civil and military offices. In many respects however, this was a hollow victory which offered little to the majority of Irishmen. More than this, the Irish Parliamentary Elections Act which accompanied the Emancipation Bill actually deprived the forty shilling freeholders of the right to vote, by raising the property qualification to £10. This move immediately cut the electorate to about one sixth of its former size.

Not alone were O'Connell's foot soldiers made pay the price for Emancipation, but further penal restrictions were actually placed on congregations of male religious. One clause of the Bill, apparently aimed at diffusing the opposition of the ultras to the measure, declared that:

> Whereas Jesuits and members of Religious Orders, Communities or Societies of the Church of Rome, bound by Monastic of Religious Vows are resident within the United Kingdom, it is expedient to make provision for the gradual suppression and final prohibition of the same therein.[12]

The Bill made it a misdemeanour for religious orders to receive new members, while any person admitted to vows was liable to banishment for life. During Lords' debate on the measure, the Prime Minister, the duke of Wellington, declared:

> There is no man more convinced than I am of the absolute necessity of carrying into execution that part of the present measure which has for its object the extinction of the Monastic Orders in this country.[13]

Whatever the intention of these penal clauses, the news of their inclusion in the Relief Bill must have appeared like a death sentence to the religious orders in Ireland.

As soon as it became known that the bill contained these provisions a meeting was called for 15 March 1829 of the regulars of Cork under the chairmanship of the Augustinian provincial, Fr Daniel O'Connor. At this meeting it was resolved to campaign against the legislation by means of memorials to parliament. Amongst the petitions presented was one from the Protestant gentry and inhabitants of the City of Waterford in favour of the Christian Brothers:

> If the members of this most useful body of men ... should come within the meaning of the Act and thereby become suppressed, it would deprive thousands of poor destitute children of education and clothing, blessings so much wanted in this country.[14]

The Cork meeting was followed by one in Dublin where Fr O'Connor and the Dominican Provincial, Fr Leahy, consulted the Regular clergy at a gathering in John's Lane Priory. At this meeting it was resolved that Edmund Rice and Fathers Leahy and O'Connor should travel to London to wait on the duke of Wellington and Robert Peel in an effort to plead their case.

This mission was unsuccessful in that the penal clauses remained, nevertheless it did serve to clarify the situation. While Wellington and Peel were both opposed to Catholic emancipation, they were certain these provisions would not be enforced against the regulars. Rice was unsatisfied with this connivance and argued with the duke that the measure was by implication casting a stigma on the religious orders: 'why should we be suppressed if we were not disloyal or obnoxious to the state?'[15] In any event, there was no way the situation could be improved; there was considerable opposition to emancipation in England and George IV had lost all patience with the Catholic question. According to Fr Leahy, Peel had suffered an outburst from the King in which he shouted: 'Damn the Catholics! Damn the Protestants! Damn you all! I can't get a moments rest about this question.'[16]

The delegation returned to Ireland without any satisfaction and Edmund Rice travelled on to Mount Sion to address a General Chapter, previously convened for 13 April 1829. Much to the surprise of the assembled brethren, Brother Rice read out his resignation to the Chapter and then withdrew. All the Brothers present were astonished; how could their founder abandon them in such critical times? They were aware that he had been ill and for some time he had been dejected; the building in North Richmond Street had been suspended for want of funds and now this crisis added to his burden. The chapter unanimously decided, successfully as it turned out, to plead with him to withdraw his resignation.

On his return, the Chapter addressed the problem of the penal clauses in the Relief Bill. Edmund read to the brothers Daniel O'Connell's opinion of the legislation, which he had given in his capacity as counsellor to the Franciscans:

> Though the law is insolent enough in its pretensions, it will be and must be totally inefficient in practice, it is almost impossible that any prosecution should be instituted at all: and it is quite impossible that any prosecution should be successful.[17]

O'Connell had also expressed a belief that the non-professed could in due course take vows without fear of prosecution. There were at that time twelve brothers who were eligible for final profession and the chapter agreed that these could be admitted immediately to perpetual vows without the usual scrutiny.

The Chapter also agreed that the Brothers would be registered in accordance with the requirements of the new law, but that the registration would be accompanied by a firm protest against the penal clause. Br Leonard's address from the Cork community was typical of the remainder:

> I hearby enter my protest against the Act, which requires free-born British subjects to submit to this mode of registering their names and professions in any office whatsoever. I deem it in every respect penal, and an infringement on the liberty and privilege of the subject, and I trust that a more enlightened Senate will erase it in common with every remnant of the penal code from the Statute Book. The persons in whose behalf this protest is made are not in orders; they are simply religious men who have voluntarily undertaken the gratuitous education of the poor neglected children of Cork.
> Cork, 15 September 1829. P.J. Leonard[18]

The Christian Brothers remained an illegal organisation until the foundation of the Irish Free State in 1922. O'Connell's interpretation of the ineffectiveness of the law was correct in the sense that the law was intended. In a broader way, however, the Brothers suffered in consequence of the law. As an illegal organisation every bequest to them was liable to be contested and there were many instances where testators' wishes were overturned. The Dublin architect Bryan Bolger, made a bequest of £10,000 to Edmund Rice and Michael (Br Bernard) Dunphy. The decision to leave the money to the named individuals was taken on legal advice in an effort to evade this penal clause. In spite of this, his nieces and nephews unsuccessfully contested the will, but after prolonged litigation the bequest frittered away to £1000. In 1839 the Commissioners of Charitable Donations and Bequests made an attempt to seize all the property bequeathed to the Brothers and were only defeated after a long legal battle in which O'Connell acted for the Brothers.[19]

IV

The 1830s brought further conflict, this time the issue at stake was the National Board of Education. Once more, Edmund proved a stalwart defendant of Catholic education, but in this instance he displayed a remarkable flexibility and total absence of obstinacy.

The 1820s had brought the question of Catholic education to a head: as 'J.K.L.' wryly remarked: 'there were not as many verse makers in Rome in the days of Horace, as there are writers and speakers on education now-a-days in a single assembly of ladies and gentlemen in Ireland'.[20] The education question had reached a climax due to a number of reasons, but

Monastery and Schools, North Richmond Street

on the Catholic side two principal factors emerged: fundamental opposition to the proselytising schools and opposition to the government sponsored Kildare Place Society.

Both of these issues were related, but Catholic opposition was most clearly focused on the latter. The educational restrictions of the eighteenth-century had led the Catholic clergy to establish their own provisional system of education. In many cases Catholic schools were simply hedge schools where the local clergy afforded a measure of patronage or supervision; in 1824, 161 of the 657 hedge schools in the Diocese of Kildare and Leighlin alone were subject to some degree of control by the local clergy.[21] In virtually all cases these parish schools were fee paying and this was necessary given the costs involved in the erection and maintenance of even the most basic school house. Free schools were generally found only in the large towns and the more prosperous counties where benefactors could provide the required capital.

The Second Reformation in the 1820s increased the sense of urgency with which the Catholic clergy viewed the education question and there was growing resentment at the levels of state funding for the Kildare Place Schools. Established in 1811, the Kildare Place Society aimed to provide a liberal education free from any imputation of proselytism. The Society intended to combine religious and secular knowledge and religious teaching consisted solely of scripture reading without comment. All catechisms and books of religious controversy were banned from their classrooms during school hours. From its foundation the Kildare Place Society received a government grant which rose to £30,000 by 1831.

Of all the educational societies, the liberal principles of the Kildare Place Society made it the most progressive. From the beginning it enjoyed a measure of Catholic support, but in the sectarian tension of the 1820s the use of scriptural texts without comment became increasingly unacceptable to the hierarchy. The 'Biblicals' had made extensive use of scriptural texts in their proselytising schools, believing that the power of the Word of God alone would be sufficient to convert the Irish. In 1820, Archbishop Troy made a specific ruling that 'the scriptures, with or without note or comment' were not fit to be used as a school-book'.[22] In the same year, John MacHale, in a series of letters under the name of *Hierophilos*, attacked Kildare Place for subsidising schools of the Biblical Societies. Later that year O'Connell, the duke of Leinster, Lord Fingal and Lord Cloncurry resigned from the Society.

The future of the Kildare Place Schools as the basis of a broad system of education was now obviously in doubt: according to Hislop, the Society was ultimately:

> A doomed experiment in 'mixed' education which ignored the realities of denominational control of schools ... The hostility which the Kildare Place experiment encountered in the 1820s proved the principle on which the Society was founded was an unworkable compromise and that the Irish education question could be solved only if the realities of denominational control, and particularly Catholic denominational control were accepted.[23]

The Catholic hierarchy now pressed the government for a solution to the educational question. In May 1824 the bishops presented parliament with a statement of the conditions under which they would accept a system of education. This pressure resulted in the establishment of a commission of inquiry to examine all aspects of educational provision in Ireland, but neither the composition of the board nor its report met with Catholic approval.

The commissioners reported in 1827 and recommended the government to discontinue its practice of channelling aid to education through voluntary agencies, such as the Kildare Place Society. Instead the commissioners advocated the establishment of a government board which would superintend a national state aided system of education. Similar recommendations were made by a parliamentary committee in 1828. The government accepted these suggestions and the chief-secretary for Ireland, Edward Stanley, outlined his plan for national education in September 1831. In the following December a seven member Board of Administration met for the first time. Two of the Board were Catholic, Bishop Murray and A.R. Blake: three were members of the Established Church,

Dr Whately, archbishop of Dublin, the duke of Leinster, and Rev. F. Sadlier, provost of Trinity College and two were Dissenters, Rev. James Carlile (Presbyterian) and Robert Holmes (Unitarian). The main features of the new system may be summarised as follows:

1. To unite in one system children of different creeds, while taking care not to interfere with the religious beliefs of any.
2. One or two days each week were to be set aside for separate religious instruction, as approved by the clergy of the different persuasions.
3. The applicants for the board's grants were given the power to appoint teachers.
4. A local contribution of not less than one third of the cost was required for building a school house. These were 'vested' schools, as opposed to 'non vested' or existing schools which joined the system
5. The board was to have complete control over the books used - schools were free to use their own texts, provided the Board approved.
6. All teachers were to be trained in a Model School in Dublin.[24]

Initially the greatest opposition to the Board came from the Protestant denominations. The Church of Ireland held a meeting in the Rotunda in January 1832 and the Primate and fifteen bishops signed a long protest at the Bill. Through the 1830s this opposition hardened and in 1838 the Church Education Society was founded to promote an alternative educational system in which all its children, Catholic and Protestant, were required to read the Bible.

The Presbyterians, too, had reservations about the system and their objections also centred on the use of scripture in class. They wished to use the Bible at any point during the day and many were inclined to exclude Catholic children while it was being read. Unlike the Church of Ireland, however, the Presbyterians sought modifications rather than a complete overthrow of the system. Following prolonged negotiations between the Synod of Ulster and the National Board an agreeable solution had been reached by 1839, whereby Catholic clergy were no longer entitled to visit non-vested schools for religious instruction.

The initial reaction of the Catholic clergy was one of quiet approval; the most vocal opposition came from John MacHale, coadjutor bishop of Killala, who believed the system was 'narrow, bigoted and insulting'.[25] Nevertheless, by 1831 the Church had been faced by an educational crisis and was unable to meet the costs of providing the necessary schools, a reality clearly illustrated in the problems faced by Edmund Rice in North

Richmond Street. The establishment of the Board seemed like an answer
to prayer: the Commissioners were prepared to fund up to two-thirds of
the cost of building and to provide texts, furniture and teachers salaries.
Besides, while Stanley had instructed the Commissioners to look with
particular favour on joint applications from different churches, he had
admitted to Archbishop Murray that joint applications would not be necessary or even likely.[26]

In effect then, the flexibility of the Commissioners assured that virtually all applications were initiated by the local parish priest and although
he undertook to fulfil all the requirements laid down by the Board, these
were in effect parish schools. Daly's analysis of the application illustrates
a high degree of continuity from the clerically patronised schools of the
1820s and the National Schools of the 1830s.[27] As one commentator has
remarked, the National System was 'the archetypal Irish solution to an
Irish problem'.[28]

For all these concessions to the Catholic cause, the National System
fell far short of the scheme outlined by Edmund Rice in 1810. Above all,
the recommendation of separate religious instruction was at total variance
with Rice's integrated approach where religion permeated the entire school
day.[29] In spite of his severe financial difficulties then, Edmund was inclined to remain independent of the National System:

Archbishop John McHale

The exclusion of the religious element he was most unwilling to grant, even for the most tempting considerations and, moreover, he was not without grave apprehension as to the injurious effect ultimately of the working of the new system to the faith of the Catholics of Ireland.[30]

Rice held many of the objections which MacHale developed at a later stage, but in response to an invitation from Archbishop Murray, he agreed to give the system a fair trial in selected schools. Accordingly Richmond Street, Mill Street, Ennis and Ennistymon were affiliated in 1833 and Waterford and Dungarvan in 1834; neither Cork, Limerick, Thurles nor Carrick-on-Suir joined the system.

The Brothers had not long to wait to see the system at variance with Edmund Rice's ideal. Most objectionable was the restriction of religious instruction to one or two days per week: prayers were said furtively and the removal of statues and the cross from class rooms caused the Brothers distress. There were also incidents where non-Catholic inspectors visited schools and mocked devotions and prayer sheets in front of the children.

The catechisms and Gahan's devotional texts, of which so much of the daily reading consisted, were banished from the school. In their place the Brothers were expected to rely on texts which they regarded as objectionable. Most of the texts were written by James Carlile, a Presbyterian minister, who modelled them on those of the Catholic Book Society. These texts, however, were not in keeping with the sentiments of the Brothers' motto, 'Catholic and Celtic, to God and Ireland true'.

Of the sixty books published by 1858, only seventeen had been written by an Irishman and of these only one, a book on gardening, was by an Irish Catholic.[31] The texts scrupulously avoided any subjects which might provoke a nationalist spirit. One commentator has observed that 'so far was the exclusion of the national spirit carried in the early days that, that in 1838 Dr Whatley struck out 'Breathes there a man with a soul so dead', and would not allow the children to hear that 'Freedom shrieked when Kosciusko fell'.[32]

Similarly in a long historical section of 130 pages in the *Fifth Book* the sole reference to Irish history was contained in a single line: 'It was towards the end of the century that Henry II of England invaded Ireland and obtained homage of the Irish kings'.[33] This ethos was again reflected in Carlile's geography lessons published in 1850. The section on the 'British Islands' begins:

The island of Great Britain, which is composed of England, Scotland, and Wales and the island of Ireland, form ... the British Empire in Europe. The people of these islands have one and the same language (all at least who are educated), one and the same laws, and though they differ in their religious worship, they all serve the same God ... All this is enough to make them brethren, in spite of many disagreements and faults which history tells ... but a better knowledge of their duty will give future history better things to record.[34]

Apart from these philosophical objections however, it must be admitted that the National Board texts were of a very high educational standard, and were well printed and illustrated. By the middle of the century these Irish school texts were the most popular in the British empire and in 1861 the royal commission on education admitted that they were the most widely used school books in England.[35]

By 1836 it was clear that the Brothers' experiment with the National Board had taken its toll. Participation in the system had a demoralising effect on the congregation, as many believed their work had been undermined by their restricted freedom to impart a Catholic education. There were other objections too, particularly from the Cork community who regarded the acceptance of state funding as a breach of the vow of gratuitous instruction. Edmund Rice had never been convinced of the value of the National system, but time had served only to confirm his doubts. He had closely monitored the progress of the communities which had been affiliated to the scheme and in 1836 convoked an extraordinary General Chapter to discuss the question of continued participation.

The Chapter met in North Richmond Street on 27 December 1836. Participation in National School systems had many advantages to offer. Most of the Brothers' communities were in dire financial circumstances; charitable donations were few and far between, while the Brothers' vows precluded them from charging even nominal fees. If nothing else, affiliation to the Board removed this difficulty. There were, however, more fundamental considerations which the Chapter believed offset any possible advantages.

The strongest opposition was directed against the prohibition of the integrated approach favoured by the Brothers. The separation of secular and religious instruction had made the latter appear of secondary importance, while the devotion to a full day each week to religion was generally regarded as impractical and educationally unsound. The fundamental contradiction between the two systems were subsequently outlined for the Powis Commission (1870):

The system of the National Board is based on a very different principle. It gives to secular instruction the first and chief place. The rules of the Board do not allow a religious emblem to be exposed in the school room, and the incidental teaching of Catholic doctrine is directly prohibited ... 'It is for Patrons and Managers to determine whether any, and if any, what religious instruction should be given in the school room', and thus practically teaching the children that religion is a matter of secondary importance and may even be laid aside altogether at discretion.[36]

The progress of the debate at the Chapter increasingly pointed to one conclusion and so it was unanimously decided that the Brothers would sever their connection with the National Board.

There were, however, serious financial restraints which made it impossible to withdraw all schools at once. Following an examination of the accounts of every foundation, Mount Sion, Richmond Street and Mill Street were withdrawn from the National System at Easter 1837. Dungarvan seceded in the following year, but it was some years before the poorer schools at Ennis (1840) and Ennistymon (1842) could be restored to their independence. Rejection of the National Board left the Brothers to their own devices in search of scarce funding, but it also alienated many friends and benefactors.

Edmund's initial decision to affiliate to the National system was, in part, out of respect for Archbishop Murray. When the difficult resolution was made to withdraw the schools Br Rice wrote informing the archbishop and concluded that 'If this step should be disagreeable to Your Grace I shall be very sorry for it'.[37] Murray was particularly displeased the Brothers' action. He was, after all, a member of the National Board, he had invested a lot in Catholic education in his diocese and been a long time benefactor of Edmund Rice's schools. Along with this, the archbishop may have felt slighted that he had not been informed of the Brothers' decision before the commissioners. In any event, Murray expressed his dissatisfaction by withdrawing an annual donation of £40 to the Hanover Street School.

The Brothers' decision to sever links with the National Board was bravely taken in difficult circumstances. Above all, it illustrated Edmund Rice's commitment to Catholic education. He had taken a front line position against the 'Biblicals' and now determined to defend the right of the poor to Catholic education. More than this, it illustrated his independence and faith in Divine Providence. While the education crisis of the 1820s forced the bishops into an unsatisfactory compromise, Edmund's confidence displayed a resilience which in time would characterise the Church he helped create.

9

Autumn

Edmund Rice's life was characterised by many contrasts. Yet there was a discernible cyclical pattern to the events of these long years. His retirement would be no different. Rather than enjoying the comfort of friends, the latter years of his life were blighted by acrimony, bitterness and recrimination. It was from these contrasts, however that Edmund had learned his favourite prayer: 'the Lord giveth, the Lord taketh away, Blessed be the Name of the Lord'. Through the trials of his retirement Edmund lived this ideal in preparation for his peaceful death in August 1844.

I

The 1830s brought a the rapid deterioration of Edmund Rice's health. Already by 1829 the trials of office had brought him to the point of exhaustion where he tendered his resignation to the General Chapter. The following decade proved equally gruelling as he faced the both the difficult experiment with the National Board and growing financial crisis. By 1835 his health had become a cause of concern but, while it was becoming clear that the burden of office was proving too much, he remained Superior General until 1838.

There were, of course, some rewarding episodes in these years. In 1835 he sent a community of Brothers to the island of Gibraltar to educate the Catholic children of the garrison there. In the following year a new school was opened in Sunderland and in 1837 further communities were established in Liverpool and Wapping. A few years later the Brothers' sister congregation established missions at Madras and Pittsburgh.

In Ireland, financial difficulties continued to frustrate Rice's plans and the plight of the Dublin houses was particularly acute. These schools survived on the proceeds of an annual charity sermon, but since 1829 there had been a marked decline in the amount raised on these occasions. Coupled with this, the Brothers' decision to withdraw from the National System in 1836 deprived them not only of the valuable grant, but also of the sympathy and support of many who did not appreciate their objections to the scheme.

By 1837 the financial position of all three Dublin houses was so critical that the only alternative to closure was the establishment of fee paying schools which could subsidise the Brothers' work amongst the poor. Br Rice had long favoured such a move, but this action was precluded by the vow of gratuitous instruction included in Pius VII's brief of approbation. Prior to 1822 the Brothers' had charged a voluntary 'fee' of one half-penny per week, but were then obliged to suspend this practice. By a unanimous decision the 1822 General Chapter unsuccessfully appealed this clause to Rome. In later years Edmund made a second appeal, but again to no avail.

In 1838 Edmund consulted Archbishop Murray on the issue and he too was enthusiastic about the proposal. Apart from guaranteeing the future of the poorer houses, fee paying schools would attract the sons of the middle class who had not previously attended the Brothers because of the stigma attached to free schools. Murray also pointed out that many

Archbishop Murray

suitable postulants might be drawn from this class.¹ In January 1838 Edmund
Rice sent a circular letter to all the perpetually professed Brothers requesting their opinion on the possible establishment of pay schools. This letter
provides a valuable insight to the plight of the Brothers' and the society in
which they lived, but it also illustrates the sharpness of Rice's mind in his
seventy-sixth year:

Dublin.
22 January, 1838.

My very dear Br ...

After serious consideration on the depressed state of some of our
houses particularly this [Nt. Richmond Street], and the impossibility of supporting others of our houses without the painful dissipat-
ing and dangerous alternative of perpetual begging even against
the wish or rather at the unpleasant expense of incurring the dis-
pleasure of Priests, and even Bishops also, the injurious effect such
a system must have on our schools, by having some of their best
conductors absent from them on this begging mission. Contemplating the impossibility of deserving support from this system on
account of the Poor Law Tax which will fall heavily on the class of
people who now contribute to our support and consequently will
absorb all they can spare, or are inclined to give, add to this the
impossibility of extending our Institute, or even adding one school
[class] to the few already established in Ireland from the circumstances of our not being in connection with the Board of Education now patronised by Bishops, Priests and Catholic Laity. These
and other such considerations lead me and other Brothers of our
Institute to the conclusion that there is but one alternative left for
the support of some of the houses already established, and the
further propagation of our Institute on a permanent and independent footing in Ireland, that is the gradual establishment of pay-
Schools for the education of the children of shop-keepers and decent
tradesmen, a class who scarcely ever receive a religious Education,
the proceeds of such schools would enable the Brothers to educate
the poor in greater numbers, and thereby counteract the effects of
a system now so popular, and which scouts religious education.

There may be some objections to what I here propose for your
consideration and in order to know the sentiments of all the professed Brothers on a matter of so much importance to our Institute,
I wish to know your and their opinion without being influenced by
any person. Another matter that strikes me and which I wish to
submit to your consideration is, the introduction of the Bible into
the National Schools, which will render it quite impossible for the

houses now in connection with the Board of Education to continue
that connection. I contemplate calling a General Chapter in order
to determine on a matter of such importance to the Institute, but I
wish beforehand to be directed by your unbiased opinion in con-
junction with those of the other professed Brs.

I remain, My very dear Br ...
Your affect. Br.,
Edmd. I. Rice.[2]

While he was awaiting the replies of the Brothers, Edmund drew up
his will and entrusted his financial affairs to three of his closest collabora-
tors, Br Francis Thornton, Br Joseph Murphy and Br Austin Dunphy.
The terms of the will were simple and his entire estate was left for the
benefit of the work and charities to which he had devoted his life. Two
years later he added two codicils to ensure that any debts he had acquired
in connection with the Institute would be honoured in full. The notable
omission from the will, however, is any allowance for the care of his
'delicate' daughter Mary, who was provided for by the Brothers until her
death in 1859.[3]

In February 1838, Edmund retired to Mount Sion. By now his health
was very poor and he was unable to administer the affairs of the Institute.
As a contemporary recalled, 'the mind and frame of our Superior were
telling against him and it became plain that he should be superseded by a
worthy successor'.[4] Accordingly he wrote to the various houses convoking
a General Chapter which would appoint his successor. Preparations were
made, delegates chosen and, following a preparatory retreat, the Chapter
opened on 24 July 1838. Edmund Rice presided over the opening proceedings and when the formalities were out of the way he addressed the
Brothers and tendered his resignation. Nine years earlier the assembled
Brothers had persuaded their founder to withdraw his resignation, but this
time all were struck by the finality of his decision.

The choice of a successor would not be easy. Edmund had led the
Brothers for thirty-six years; many of the congregation had joined with
the specific intention of following his example. The cult of his personality, the quality of his leadership and his renowned holiness all contributed
to make the choice of successor exceedingly difficult. The correct choice
was imperative since, according to the terms of rescript granted to the
Institute by Pope Gregory XVI in 1832, the new Superior General would
serve for life. The Brothers had never before been in the position of
having to chose a Superior General; they were unfamiliar with the proce-
dure and there was no obvious choice to succeed Br Rice. Accordingly the
first four ballots were inconclusive and the election of Br Paul Riordan on

a controversial fifth ballot required a subsequent *senatio* from Rome to confirm its validity.

There was a moving episode that evening at supper, which was later recalled by Brother Stephen Carroll, a novice at the time:

> The same day when the bell rang for dinner I was present in the dining room and the ex-Superior was one of the first to enter, and he stood right by the side of his chair which he filled for many a long year. As the newly elected walked in the ex-Superior said to him 'this, Sir, is your seat'. I heard him say so, and obliged him to sit therein, then and there.[5]

Following the election of the new General the Chapter returned to the thorny issue of pay schools. The chapter was bitterly divided on the point, with the greatest opposition to the plan coming from Paul Riordan and the Brothers of the North Monastery. Normoyle argues that all of the capitulants were committed to the education of the poor as their principal duty, but that their attitude towards the proposed pay schools depended to a large extent on the financial position of the houses in which they lived. The Brothers in England, for instance, had free accommodation, heating and an average stipend of £50 per annum. The North Monastery, Br Riordan's community, lived equally securely on the proceeds of a substantial bequest made to the school in 1835.[6]

Positions were difficult to reconcile and debate continued through the 5th, 6th, 7th and 12th session of the chapter. It was only in the final session that a resolution was achieved, and this ultimately proved unsatisfactory. By way of a compromise, the chapter declared its opposition *in principle* to pay-schools, but on account of dire necessity agreed to allow the Brothers at Mill Street and Hanover Street charge nominal fees. Having reached this difficult decision, the chapter was dissolved, but before the Brothers went their separate ways, they each paid homage to the man who had brought them together.

II

The transfer from founder to successor is inevitably a difficult transition. In the case of the Irish Christian Brothers it was a particularly acrimonious affair. The new Superior General, Paul Riordan, a native of Clonmel, was forty nine years of age at the time of his election. Before joining the Institute he was employed as a clerk in the counting house of a Cork silk merchant and frequently travelled to France and Spain on business. In 1822, he joined the Brothers in the North Monastery and he lived there until his election as Superior General sixteen years later. Consequently, his experience of the Congregation was very limited. Cork had not experienced the difficulties which had beset the other communities and he failed to appreciate many of his predecessor's preoccupations and policies. This brought him into league with the two Brothers Leonard in his community and together they formed an anti-Rice faction in the congregation.

Perhaps the election of Brother Dunphy, Edmund's closest collaborator, would have made the transition of power more agreeable, but the choice of his staunchest critic created bitter tension. Rice had provided the Institute with strong, charismatic leadership; Paul Riordan found it difficult living in his shadow and made no secret of it.[7] There were a number of tragic clashes between the two, in which Edmund was forced to endure insult and humiliation.

By 1840 the school in North Richmond Street was, once again, in serious financial circumstances. Some of the Brothers, including Rice, believed the situation to be so critical that only mortgaging the school would secure its future. Riordan strongly opposed this proposal and strictly forbade the Brothers under obedience from proceeding with their plan. Edmund, whose name was on the deeds of the school, sought advice from R.J. Colgan, the distinguished Carmelite theologian. It was Colgan's opinion that 'no subject was bound to obey his superior commanding anything sinful or contrary to justice'. Since the repayment of debts was involved, Rice felt obliged to proceed with his proposal and duely mortgaged the school in July 1840.[8] Edmund was nevertheless troubled by the decision to defy his superior, but explained to Archbishop Murray that 'I have done no more in this affair than justice called upon me to do'.[9]

Br Riordan failed to appreciate Edmund's motivation and adopted a petty, vindictive attitude towards his predecessor. In the summer of 1840 Br Rice paid a visit to the community at Hanover Street where his friend Austin Dunphy was superior. The Brothers there had no spare bed and requested one for their founder from the generalate at Richmond Street. In spite of the many beds available in that house, which he had built and furnished himself, Edmund Rice suffered the humiliation of having this simple request refused.

Relations between the two were further soured in July 1840 when a group of Brothers petitioned the Holy See for the deposition of Riordan. Included amongst the 'signatures' was that of 'Edmd. Rice, the humble instrument under divine Providence in founding this society'.[10] The signature was subsequently exposed as a forgery, but it is surprising that Br Rice was never formally challenged about his signing the memorial to Rome. In any event the episode served to further isolate Edmund and he lost a great deal of support through the whole affair. One of his oldest friends, Fr Peter Kenny S.J., declared:

I found that my conscientious conviction forced me to disapprove of the very men who were my own greatly revered friends and old acquaintances. I have been in close habits of sacred friendship with good Mr Rice for nine and thirty years, and the part he has taken with the memorialists is the only fault I had ever to complain of.[11]

For Br Riordan this provided another opportunity to undermine his predecessor. Writing to Paul Cullen, Rector of the Irish College in Rome, in 1842, he dismissed the whole affair, attributing it simply to Rice's senility:

I do not by any means censure the Ex-Supr. for the part he has taken in these disedifying matters, as he had been labouring imbecility of mind for some time before he went out of office and has been ever since.[12]

In 1841, Rice suffered the final bitter indignity of being turned away from the door of a chapter of the Institute he had founded, and which had been called by Br Riordan in an effort to reconcile differences.

III

As Edmund's health failed he was increasingly confined to his beloved Mount Sion. Away from the politics and bickering Edmund lived out his last days to the full. Age had not dimmed his interest in the school and while he was able to move about he would visit the class rooms to encourage both masters and boys. One of the Brothers later recalled such visits:

When he entered my school it was my custom to get a seat for him, and he would sit down and look at the work with great pleasure. He would speak in his own kindly and affable manner to the groups of reverent youngsters who would invariably try to get as near as possible to him whom they loved as a father and revered as a saint. They would come to present him their writing copies, and go away delighted with a word of approbation. His pleasure in hearing the little ones say the prayers and answer the catechism was delightful to observe'.[13]

One of the pupils had equally fond memories of these visits. Years later, Patrick Browne remembered how the 'boys had such a veneration for Brother Rice that they regarded it even as a privilege to get a look at him. Though he was reserved in his manner towards them he was ever kind in his intercourse with them'.[14]

Accompanied by a Brother he would walk through the grounds of Mount Sion. Inevitably, he would encourage his young helper to greater devotion to the Blessed Virgin. One of these helpers, Br Aloysius Hoare, remembered the advice he was given: 'Have great devotion to Our Blessed Lady; say in her honour the *Memorare* and she will take care of you and obtain for you the crowning grace of final perseverance'.[15] Edmund retained his interest in spiritual reading and when his sight failed he would have the novices read for him. He would frequently request to hear some passages about heaven and would say 'How easy to die', and sometimes 'O God, did we even now rightly begin to serve you, your loving heart would take us all to its final embrace'.[16]

At Christmas 1841 his health again failed and there seemed to be no hope of recovery. Br Paul Riordan notified the various communities of their founder's condition:

> With feelings of pain and sorrow I have to inform you that our most dear Br. Ignatius Rice has been unusually ill since Christmas Eve. He has no pain or uneasiness, but great weakness, which confines him to his bed, and will, it is feared, end in his dissolution. I request you will have the prayers of the community offered, to beg for him the grace of a happy death.[17]

Contrary to expectations he rallied for a short while and was able to attend to his personal correspondence. The long term indications, however, were not good and before long he was confined to his room. In time his mental faculties began to fail and he lived his last days in a semi-coma; from May 1842 he required the constant attention of a nurse. So regular had the pattern of prayer been through his life that, even though he appeared unaware of what he was saying, his first words on awakening each morning were 'Praise be to you, O Christ'.[18]

In August 1844 Edmund's health showed signs of rapid deterioration. On the morning of August 28 he was anointed by his confessor and the Brothers joined in prayerful vigil around his bedside. Amongst those present was a young novice, Br Stanislaus Hyland, who treasured the memory of his last meeting with Edmund Rice:

> I was sent to Mount Sion, Waterford, in 1844 to prepare for Profession, and there was the Founder, my revered Superior, fast drawing to an end. Mine was the last hand, I think, that he shook in friendship on this earth.
>
> I had just returned from St Patrick's branch school, and I at once ran up to see him. He clasped my hand in his, now clammy before death. I noticed his clasp growing unconsciously closer, and a doze seemed to come on. His eye was glassy. I was expecting the bell to ring for dinner, and I said aloud to him: 'Good bye, Sir; the bell will soon ring'. I disengaged my hand from his grasp, and he awoke and said to me: 'Good bye, and God Bless you, my child'.[19]

Edmund died the following morning, 29 August. Describing the late General, Br Joseph Murphy, Superior of Mount Sion, wrote: 'his life was a long series of sufferings, labours and contradictions under which he manifested a greatness of soul which betokened sublime virtue'.[20]

The communities of the Institute were duly notified of the sad news of his passing:

> We have the sorrowful duty of announcing to you the death of our most dear Father, Founder, and Brother, Ignatius Rice, who died at eleven o'clock this morning after having received the Last Sacrament.
>
> We trust he is gone to receive the reward of his labour for the poor, for the Congregation, and for us all.[21]

Edmund's body was dressed in the habit of the Congregation, with beads and a crucifix in his hands, and placed in the small oratory at Mount Sion. The Brothers prayed by his side and a great number of people came to pay their last respects. The Mayor and the leading citizens of the city, together with parents and pupils, came and knelt beside the remains of the great benefactor of the poor of Waterford.

The *Waterford Mail* announced Edmund's death and described him in glowing terms as:

> A venerable, a good, and, in the best sense of the word, a great man ... A man of vast knowledge of human nature, of a comprehensive grasp of intellect, of indomitable energy, of irresistible perseverance, of unbending integrity, of profoundest piety, of boundless charity, Edmund Rice, the Founder of the Christian Brothers, is dead—the herald of a new age to Irishmen in education, the harbinger of virtue and of blessings, and the benefactor of his fellowmen in every country where his brothers have been established.[22]

On Saturday, 31 August, Bishop Nicholas Foran presided at the Solemn Requiem Mass and final obsequies at Mount Sion. He was joined on the altar by twenty-nine priests and the small oratory was filled to capacity with Christian Brothers and the leading citizens of Waterford. After the Mass his remains were interred in the cemetery of the monastery grounds and the spot was marked by a simple stone cross.

The restricted capacity of the oratory at Mount Sion made the exclusion of the public from the obsequies unavoidable, but the Bishop of Waterford set aside October 1, the 'Month's Mind', for a great public thanksgiving for the life of Edmund Rice. This occasion was marked by a High Mass in the city's splendid cathedral, where the seats were removed

Edmund Rice

to accommodate the huge crowd. Dr Foran presided at the ceremony and was joined on the altar by fifty priests, including the Apostle of Temperance, Fr Mathew, who travelled from Cork for the occasion. Among the Christian Brothers who assembled to pay their respects to their Founder were thirty five members of the Congregation from the schools in England. The oration was delivered by Fr Richard Fitzgerald, chaplain to Mount Sion, and he summed up the great achievement of Edmund Rice:

> Need I say that he stands not in need of the genius of the sculptor or the painter; for as long as gratitude shall find a place in the Irish heart, as long as religion shall be prized, as long as sterling patriotism shall be accounted a virtue, the name of Edmund Ignatius Rice shall be held in benediction.[23]

10

Modernisation

Rice's life spanned a crucial era, from the dawn of Emancipation to the eve of the Great Famine. These were critical years in the formation of Catholic consciousness, marking the emergence from the penal era and the establishment of the modern church. In all of this Rice made a significant contribution, fostering confidence and creating a literate modern working class. Rice's spirituality was characterised by an unyielding faith in Divine Providence. Yet he was a man of immense practicality who channelled his energies towards the provision of education for the poor. In so doing, Edmund played a vital role in the modernisation of Irish society, a contribution which is often forgotten in the tendency to portray his successors as reactionaries, hell-bent on the defence of 'faith and fatherland'.

I

The late eighteenth and early nineteenth-centuries saw the emergence of the Catholic Church in Ireland from the restrictions of the penal laws. Modern writing has clearly illustrated that the story of the Church during the penal era was one of endurance and emergence rather than the traditionally accepted image of unrelenting persecution. This revival, however, was uneven in many respects. The obvious differences were geographical, where the recovery was most pronounced in mid-Munster/south-Leinster and renewal percolated only slowly into Ulster/north-Connacht. In social terms too, contrary to the received image, Catholicism as an institutional force was more firmly entrenched in the richer areas, the upper social classes and the towns.

These factors are clearly illustrated in the case of Edmund Rice and the religious founders of the period. It was from their class, the strong farmer/merchant ranks, that the great impetus for renewal came. They were the driving force behind the spate of chapel building which characterised the period, while they also tackled the problem of Catholic education. This was a closely knit group, sharing many common connections: the Jesuit Peter Kenney, for instance, was spiritual director to both Edmund Rice and Teresa Ball the foundress of the Irish Loreto Sisters. Edmund

Rice was inspired by the work of Nano Nagle and she in turn was related to Edmund Burke, the great champion of Catholic emancipation, and Fr Theobald Mathew, the Apostle of Temperance.

At an institutional level, Edmund Rice's financial acumen facilitated the great religious revival. For years he acted as financial advisor to the Presentation Sisters, investing their dowries, managing their accounts and assisting in the acquisition of property. There is a tradition too, that Edmund managed the finances of the suppressed Jesuit Order until their restoration in 1814. Certainly his letter to Peter Kenney, the new provincial, on the opening of Clongowes Wood College in 1814 indicates that he was very familiar with all aspects of the ownership of that property.[1] Edmund also acted for the bishops of Ireland, purchasing government bonds and stock on their behalf.

Amongst the urban poor, the Christian Brothers and the teaching Sisters played a vital part in widening the base of the institutional Church. Through their teaching and catechetical instruction the Brothers introduced the poor to the new forms of Catholic devotion which became the hallmark of nineteenth-century Catholicism. The effect of this teaching was to bring a previously alienated class within the ranks of the Church, which in time provided the backbone of the emerging Catholic Ireland.

On another level too, the Brothers created an urban working class. Just as the Methodists in England and Wales transformed society, so the Brothers in Ireland instilled in their pupils the virtues of discipline, hard-work and sobriety.[2] From the very beginning Edmund Rice cultivated these values. Charles Bianconi, one of the first recipients of Edmund's charity, was encouraged to be 'sedulous and industrious', careful and sober.[3] These values were at the core of the Brother's programme and were celebrated by contemporary commentators. The *Waterford Chronicle*, in June 1816, hailed the work at Mount Sion:

> They have withdrawn multitudes from the dangers of idleness and vice, and have reared them in the pursuit of useful knowledge and in the habits of virtuous and honourable industry.[4]

Dean Ryland of Christ Church expressed similar praise for the work of the Christian Brothers:

> They have already impressed upon the lower classes a character which hitherto was unknown to them: and in the number of intelligent and respectable tradesmen, clerks and servants which they have sent forth, bear the most unquestionable testimony to the public services of Edmund Rice.[5]

The Brothers played a vital role in the formation of this disciplined work force. Their curriculum was constructed so as to meet the employment demands of nineteenth-century industrial society. Great emphasis was placed on literacy in English: Edmund Rice consciously placed clocks in class rooms 'to better direct them in regulating the time', and the syllabus included modern subjects, 'calculation, good writing and a thorough knowledge of book-keeping'.[6] Referring to the opening of Mount Sion, Edmund's biographer has written:

> The good work initiated on that first day of May 1804 coincided with the dawn of the moral, intellectual and religious regeneration of the youth of Ireland.[7]

All of these factors point to Edmund Rice's inclusion in the great modernisation process which swept the nineteenth-century world. Fifteen years ago H.F. Kearney published a seminal article in which he argued that Fr Mathew should rightly be celebrated as 'the Apostle of Modernisation'.[8] He believed the temperance crusade was only intelligible within a transatlantic context, beginning in New England in the 1820s and gradually spreading to Britain and Ireland. Far from being simply a tee-total campaign, this was part of a wider process of modernisation and was linked with other campaigns, including the abolition of slavery. Thackery described Fr Mathew as:

> Avoiding all political questions, no man seems more eager than he for the political improvement of this country. Leases and rents, farming implements, reading societies, he was full of these and his schemes of temperance above all.[9]

The campaign was modernising, too, Kearney argues, in the sense that it represented a shift from 'local' to 'cosmopolitan' values and an attempt by urban men to control and reform rural society:

> The urban thrust of the crusade, its emphasis upon such values as literacy, thrift, and insurance against illness and its involvement in politics in some areas link it to other movements which were attempting to cope with the new problems of a changing world.[10]

It is surprising, however, that Kearney and both of Fr Mathew's recent biographers have neglected the crucial part played by Edmund Rice in this campaign for temperance and modernisation.[11]

Sobriety had been a constant theme in Edmund's teaching. Of the few anecdotes which survive about him one of the most substantial concerns a

Waterford alcoholic and 'lady of the lane', Poll McCarthy, who begged
Edmund for help. Instead of listening to her tales of woe, he lectured her
on her drinking. She promised that if he would help her, she would go to
Cork and take the pledge from Fr Mathew. There and then he brought
her to a drapers and fitted her for the journey. She walked to Cork and
back and 'her life subsequently was as edifying as previously it had been
notorious'.[12]

Within the schools, too, he encouraged temperance. Many of the *Memoirs*
of Edmund Rice recall his kindness to the children of alcoholics; how he
took special care of them, while at the same time seeking out their parents
and urging them 'to lead a better more sober life'.[13] Another remembered
how he had established a Purgatorial Society at Mount Sion, where he
lectured the people on matters which promoted temperance.[14] This, in
fact, may be a reference to the juvenile temperance society founded at
Mount Sion by Br. P.J. Murphy who in time became one of Fr Mathew's
most devoted lieutenants.

Edmund Rice and Fr Mathew were friends for over forty years; the
friendship may have begun while the young Mathew was a pupil at St
Canice's Academy in Kilkenny, before he went to Maynooth in 1800.
Both men shared a common vision and desire to improve the lot of the
poor. Education was also a concern of the young Capuchin; shortly after
arriving in Cork in 1814 he established a school in an effort to do for the
south side what the Brothers had done for the north. By 1824 there were
500 pupils in this school and before the Brothers' school at Sullivan's
Quay was completed in 1828, classes were held in an old store at Cove
Street, where Fr Mathew lived.[15]

The Brothers played a crucial part in Fr Mathew's temperance crusade
and both movements were closely identified. The first juvenile total absti-
nence society founded in Ireland was at the North Monastery and Fr
Mathew consciously cultivated contacts with the Brothers. In June 1843,
in North Richmond Street, he praised the work of the Brothers and
expressed his delight:

> That the Christian Brothers had come forward as living examples
> of the great lessons of total abstinence which they inculcated. He
> thanked God that he had their active co-operation and that of their
> numerous pupils whose example alone in taking the pledge was a
> vast gain for the cause of temperance.[16]

Later in the same year he described the day Edmund Rice took the
pledge as the happiest day of his life:

> I was aware that when he and the other members of that illustrious

body came forward from their mountain, a second Carmel, to diffuse the blessings of temperance as they had those of education, not only through Ireland, but also in England, the principles of the Society were placed on a sure basis, even on a rock which the breaking of the tempest could not shake.[17]

The identification of the cause of education and temperance found expression in Fr Mathew's numerous visits to the Brothers' schools. In 1843 alone, he made at least nine visits to their schools; in September of that year he delivered a charity sermon for the North Richmond Street school in Gardiner Street church which raised one hundred guineas. In 1845, when Daniel O'Connell visited the North Monastery the hall was decorated with two large satin banners; one read *in hoc signo vinces*, while 'Temperance and happiness' was emblazoned on the other.[18]

In late January 1844 Fr Mathew visited Edmund Rice for the last time at Mount Sion. Ten months later he sat next to Bishop Foran at the great

Fr Mathew

month's mind Mass in the cathedral of Waterford. According to Fr Mathew's biographer, the month's mind was originally planned for 2 October, but was held a day earlier in order that the 'Apostle of Temperance', who was due to preach at the consecration of Dun Laoire Church, could attend.[19] Given this close kinship and the effective role played by the Brothers in the process of modernisation it is surprising that Fr Mathew's recent biographers have failed to make even a passing reference to Br Rice.

II

The forthcoming beatification of Edmund Rice will inevitably focus attention on his life and deeds. The absence of a diary, memoirs or a contemporary biographer restrict our image of the man's personality to mere glimpses. Above all, his modesty and reticence make him an elusive subject for a biographer. His contemporaries, for instance, appear to have been unaware of the most basic details about his short marriage. Edmund's modesty was extreme: on one occasion the Brothers requested him to sit for a portrait, 'for what', he replied, 'so as you can look at it while I'm in Purgatory'. Fortunately, the General Chapter of 1841 directed Brothers who had known Rice to record their recollections and it is from this archive that our best insights are drawn.

His correspondence, too, tends to be practical and business like and this provides but a few glimpses on the life of his soul. There is, however, one inspiring letter written to the Dublin architect Bryan Bolger in which he reveals something of his inspiration:

> Let us do ever so little for God, we will be sure He will never forget it, nor let it pass unrewarded. How many of our actions are lost for want of applying them to this end. Were we to know the merit of only going from one street to another to serve a neighbour for the love of God, we should prize it more than gold or silver ... One thing you may be sure of, that whilst you work for God, whether you succeed or not, he will amply reward you.[20]

There is also a sense visible in his correspondence and actions that he constantly strove against the natural inclination of his family and class. The isolation of the texts against usury may suggest qualms of conscience, while his generosity to the poor was in stark contrast to the acquisitive nature attributed to his family. Occasionally the preoccupations of his class became visible in his frequent recourse to the law to secure tenure or bequests, but in these instances it was the poor, rather than himself, who stood to benefit from litigation.

Above all, Edmund's life is characterised by a remarkable perseverance and faith in divine providence. Writing on the centenary of his death in 1944, Archbishop John Charles McQuaid wrote, 'it is this character of initial failure and mighty renaissance which strikes one in considering the life and work of Edmund Ignatius Rice'.[21] Similar sentiments were contained in the report of the theologians to the Sacred Congregation for the Causes of Saints presented in 1992:

> A man can be patient when there is nothing to drive him to anger and bitterness. We can all thank God for the weather when the sun is shining and the birds are singing. For Edmund Rice it is not clear that the birds were ever singing in balmy sunshine; it seemed to be mostly gales and hail and rain. Constant financial problems, cholera, political pressures, the nasty scheming of officials, opposition from some bishops and priests. All these he might have allowed for, but if he had not read the lives of the saints he might not have been prepared for the bitter opposition from his own brothers and the painful disharmony among them. Yet his serenity was unruffled and his trust in divine providence unabated whatever happened to him or his work.[22]

Appendices

APPENDIX ONE: TEXTS AGAINST USURY

Ex 22:25   If you lend money to any of my people that is poor, that dwelleth with thee: thou shalt not be hard on upon them as an extortioner, nor oppress them with usuries.

Lev 25:35-6   If thy brother be impoverished, and weak of hand, and thou receive him as a stranger and sojourner, and he live with thee: Take not usury of him nor more than thou gagest. Fear thy God, they thy brother may live with thee.

Dt 23:19   Thou shalt not lend to thy brother money to usury, nor corn, nor any other thing.

Ps 14:5   He that hath not put out his money to usury, nor taken bribes against the innocent; he that doth these things shall not be moved for ever.

Ps 54: 11-12   Day and night shall iniquity surround it upon its walls; and in its midst thereof are labour and injustice. And usury and deceit have not departed from its streets.

Prov 22:16   He that oppresseth the poor, to increase his own riches, shall himself give to one that is richer, and shall be in need.

Prov 28:8   He that heapeth together riches by usury and loan gathereth them for him that will be bountiful to the poor.

Ez 18:31   That grieveth the needy and the poor: that taketh away by violence: that restoreth not the pledge: and that lifteth up his eyes to idols: that committeth abomination: that giveth up usury and that taketh an increase; shall such a one live? He shall not live.

Ez 18:31   Cast away from you all your transgressions, by which you
             have transgressed, and make to yourselves a new heart and
             a new spirit: and why should you die, O House of Israel?

2 Esd 5:11   Restore ye to them this day their fields, and their hundreth
             part of the money, and of the corn, the wine and the oil,
             which you were wont to exact from them, give it rather for
             them.

Mt 5:42   Give to him that asketh of thee; and from him that would
             borrow of thee turn not away.

Lk 6:35   But love ye your enemies; do good and lend, hoping for
             nothing thereby; and your reward shall be great and you
             shall be the sons of the highest for he is kind to the unthankful
             and to the evil.

APPENDIX TWO: EDMUND RICE
TO THE ARCHBISHOP OF CASHEL

My Lord,

I should have sent the enclosed regulations of our schools to Yr. Grace
before now, but waiting for an opportunity of some person going to Thurles,
—Yr. Grace I hope will be able to select something out of them for to save
the school of Thurles. The half-hour's explanation of the Catechism I
hold to be the most salutary part of the system. It is the most laborious to
the teachers; however, if it were ten times what it is, I must own we are
amply paid in seeing such a Reformation in the Children—Drs Moylan &
McCarthy have sent two young men to serve a Noviceship for the purpose
of establishing our Institute in Cork. I trust in the goodness of God that it
will spread before long in most parts of the Kingdom—indeed it would
give me particular satisfaction to see it prosper in Thurles—May God
give Your Grace life to see this effected. Anything in our power to serve
this purpose Yr. Grace can freely command.

                                          I am, My Lord
                        Your Grace's Most Obt. & Humble Servant
                                              Edmd. Rice.
                                      Waterford 9 May 1810.

Source: Normoyle, *A Tree is Planted*, pp 30-1.

Enclosure

Our schools open at nine o'clock in the morning at which time the business of the Masters who attend immediately commences. The boys whom we instruct are divided. Those who are advanced, so as at least to be able to read tolerably well, with others who are taught arithmetic, etc., occupy an upper room. The lower room is for such as are taught spelling, reading and writing on slates. In the upper room the boys are arranged as much as may be, according to their degrees of improvement, at double desks 12 on each. Over each desk a monitor or superintendent is appointed, who keeps An account of the conduct of those committed to his care—that they are at school in due time, diligently attend their school duties, etc. The desks are divided into different districts each of which is committed to the care of a master.

In the morning, the monitors of the several districts prepare the copy books of the boys under their care, and bring them to their respective masters, top have copy lines written or pieces to write from—pens prepared for writing, etc. While the boys wait for the copy books they are employed in looking over the tasks for the day. The writing of the copies usually commences as much as may be at the sametime, that the masters may visit their respective desks, and give particular instructions relative to writing properly, and according to approved methods.

After the copies are written, Reading Lessons commence, the boys of each desk coming up according to their turn. The books made use of are Gahan's *History of the New and Old Testament.* Comments are made, and familiar moral instructions are given the class in the course of the lesson by the master. Whilst one class reads and hears instruction, the other desks are employed at sums, etc. At a convenient time the monitors question the boys of their desks in spelling and catechism tasks and make reports to the masters accordingly.

At the half hour before twelve o'clock the bell rings for giving general moral instructions, at which time one of the masters whose turn it is, having the boys all assembled about him, explains the Catechism or out of *Gobinet*, or other books that are deemed fit, gives instructions suited to the capacity of the children.

When the clock strikes twelve the Angelus and Acts of Faith, Hope and Charity with a few other devotional prayers are recited, after which the boys are dismissed and the school closes until one. At one, school opens again and from that to three the exercises are similar to those of the morning as nearly as time will admit. At three, the Litany of the Blessed Virgin, Salve Regina and a few other prayers are recited, when the boys are dismissed and school closes for the day. They are not allowed to play or keep company with any other boys but those of the school when out of it.

The children in the lower school are arranged in classes according to their degree of improvement as in the upper room. Those who write on slates at desks, the others on forms or other convenient seats. The desks are single, seven boys range at each and every boy provided with a slate to write on. Monitors are appointed for the desks as before mentioned whose duties are similar. Such assistants in fact are found so necessary that they are made use of even down to the lowest classes.

The masters who attend, commence the business of the morning by writing copies for the classes committed to their care. The copyline for the boys of a desk is the same, they being arranged, as before remarked, so that those who are nearly equal in improvement and abilities are kept together.

Each class writes the copy set them 4 or 5 times over without getting the copyline changed and always when finished requests the master to inspect them, and according to his decision inflict slight punishments on each other for defects in their writing—a permission given them for the purpose of stimulating one another to proper exertions. The masters give instructions in spelling, reading etc., occasionally, so that the boys may at least get two lessons; they are besides questioned in spelling and Catechism tasks by the master or the monitor if found fit.

Familiar moral instructions are given occassionally at the time of reading or otherwise by the masterts who attend this school, suited to the weak capacity of those under their care. But no general instructions as in the upper room; the time appointed for that purpose being employed in teaching prayers and Catechism to the most ignorant. At twelve the Angelus etc., as above, after which they are dismissed till one. From one till three the exercises are the same as in the morning.

N.B. The slates that the boys write on, are ruled on one side with a sharp pointed piece of iron so that an impression is thereby made on the slate, and that thus when they have an occasion to blot out or deface any letter that they wish to improve, or the entire copy, the ruling remains. The other side is left for sums, etc., and of course is not ruled.

General examinations of the copies, sums, etc., are made twice a week in the upper school room, and rewards and punishments dealt out accordingly. More general ones are held two or three times a year, and such as are found most deserving receive gifts proportioned to their merit. Each boy reads about a page and a half, while the others of his desk stand with him when necessary. The half hour for instruction is given on Fridays for a general examination of the Catechism. Unless for some faults which rarely occur whipping is never inflicted.

A boy who has the care of about one hundred and fifty pious books, most of which are numbered, on every Friday evening distributes them amongst the monitors of each desk, of which he makes an entry; and they are obliged to return them to the boy giving a choice to the most deserving of which he also takes an account, by this regulation we seldom lose a book. We also supply the boys who are bound out to apprentices, with pious books, who are in general obliged to go to Sacraments once a month; and some are allowed by their Confessor to go more frequent.

The confessions of all the children are heard every year on 15th July, 15th Oct., 15th Jan., and 15th April, provided nothing interfered on those days to prevent it in which case it is defered to another day. The boys read books for their parents at night, and on Sundays and Holydays, and instruct them otherwise when they can do it with prudence, from which we find much good to result.

We have a clock in the school, the better to direct them in the regulating the time, and every time it strikes, silence is observed all over the schools, and every boy blesses himself, says the Hail Mary, and makes some short pious aspirations which continues about a minute when they bless themselves again and resume their business.

Source: Cashel Diocesan Archives, Normoyle, *Companion*, pp. 1-5.

APPENDIX THREE: EDMUND RICE'S OBITURARY AS APPEARED IN THE CORK EXAMINER OF 9 SEPTEMBER 1844

DEATH OF EDMOND IGNATIUS RICE
(From the *Tipperary Vindicator*)

The Waterford papers announce the death of a venerable, a good, and, in the best sense of the word, a great man—a man of powerful mind—of vast knowledge of human nature—of a comprehensive grasp of intellect—of undaunted courage—of irrestible perseverance—of unbending integrity—of pure piety—of immense charity—Edmond Rice, the founder of Christian Schools—the herald of a new age of Irishmen in the way of instruction—the harbinger of virtue and of blessings—the benefactor of his species, not only in Ireland but in whatever quarter of the globe the present generation of the humbler classes of our fellow countrymen have penetrated, because to Mr. Rice is mainly attributable the credit of whatever intellectual training they enjoy. We regret our Waterford contemporaries have confined their notice of the loss of this inestimable man to a simple paragraph.—The following are the words of the announcement in the Mail and the Chronicle:—

'At Mount Sion, in this city, in the 87th year of his age, the venerable Brother Edmond Ignatius Rice, founder of the Brothers of the Christian Schools in Ireland and England. The health of this venerable man has been declining for nearly three years. He bore his protracted illness with patience and resignation to the Divine will. In this city he founded his first establishment for the gratuitous education of boys in the year 1803, which has since branched out to the principal towns in this country and England. He was a man of indefatigable zeal and charity, endowed with great prudence, energy, and perseverance. He resigned the office of superior-general of his institute in the year 1838, in order to give his undivided attention to the concerns of his immortal soul. The city of Waterford particularly has lost in him one of its best benefactors.'

We regret that those who are on the spot have not been able to contribute more particulars of the life and exertions of this truly excellent man. We have had opportunities of knowing and appreciating his exalted work—of witnessing in some degree the extent and value of his labours—of being partially acquainted with the strength and depth of the magnificent edifice which he raised for the instruction of the children of the poor of his native city in the first instance, and of Ireland, almost universally, afterwards. We have had some means of judging of the vast advantages conferred upon society by his ceaseless toils. We would endeavour, therefore to supply the void left by our Waterford contemporaries, to whom we should have looked for the minutest particulars connected with the subject.

Mr. Rice, as appears from the paragraph above given, had arrived at the middle period of life before he founded the Christian schools, he was in fact forty six years of age at the time. But for some years before he was engaged in planning the system, whose maturity he enjoyed the gratification of witnessing, and whose triumph is one of the most remarkable features in the modem history of Ireland. In 1803 he commenced an establishment in Waterford, for the gratuitous instruction of youth in literature and Christian piety. He was joined in the undertaking by two young men, desirous of devoting their lives to the same laudable purposes. In May, 1804, during the episcopacy of the Right Rev. John Power, a prelate whose memory is held in deserved reverence to this day in Waterford, the schools were opened. We are not exactly informed of the causes that operated on the mind of Mr. Rice to take this step. It was a new—it must have been a hazardous one just then. The great mass of the people were utterly unacquainted with even the rudiments of learning. The country had been suffering from the effects of the rebellion of 1798—the mad rebellion of the unfortunate Emmet only broke out. The achievements of Napoleon were attracting universal concern, and causing general alarm. We believe that Mr. Rice's early life had not given promise of that religious seriousness which he now began to display. He had been engaged in trade—if we be not incorrect, it was in the provision trade—then one of the principal branches of business in Waterford, where, though the export of beef is annihilated, that of bacon, even at this day, is greater than from any other port of Ireland. His avocations classes. He perceived their igno-rance—he perceived that brought him into immediate contact with the working in many instances irreligion proceeded from their ignorance—and that to its prevalence much of the crime that abounded could also be traced. He lived in a part of the city where vice and ignorance prevailed to a greater extent than elsewhere. En passant, we may observe that about this time also Mr. Rice had a brother in Cadiz who occasionally lived in San Lucin de Berramueda and Seville, and who was also engaged in trade; he, too, abandoned the desk for the cloister. became an Augustinian friar, and by his abilities, energy, and piety, did vast service to his order in Ireland; he lived for many years in Callan, and died some years ago in Malta, to which place he went from Rome on business connected with his order. Mr. Rice having once embarked in the cause he undertook was resolved to persevere; he did not mind the difficulties that opposed his progress—every obstacle tended but to give him more nerve—he was determined to work out the great achievement on which he had set his heart. He and his associates, few, but zealous, proceeded success—fully in their good work. Daily augmentations were made to the numbers that flocked to their schools. They could have had no better cradle for their infant instruction than Waterford, where the purest piety and unbounded charity have always been known to exist, and where a princely magnifi-cence on the part of the citizens in forwarding every benevolent object has always been known to prevail. It was but a few years before, and just when they were permitted by law, that the citizens erected one of the noblest edifices ever raised in this country to the worship of God, and one which has not since been surpassed in Ireland. The acute (eulogium, and great was the compliment coming from judgement of the learned Dr. Milner passed upon the facade of the Catholic cathedral of Waterford a high the accomplished historian of Winchester cathedral, though Mr. Pagin is said to have expressed himself differently on a recent occasion. Mr. Rice and his companions attracted the attention of pious and benevolent citizens. Paul Carroll—a name which shall never be forgotten in Waterford—aided their incipient efforts, as he kntw how to do. Thomas O'Brien, an eminent wine merchant—one of the good old times—a gentleman in the purest acceptation of the term, appreciated the good they performed, founded a school and establishment at his own expense in Carrick-on-Suir, of which town we believe he was a native, and this with the approbation of Dr. Power.

The school was finished in 1807, and is now one of the best of the description in Ireland, presided over for many years by a truly religious and good man, who has done material service to the community. In the same year, Dungarvan participated in a similar advantage. The school in Dungarvan had been for many years situated outside the town, at a place called Shandon; it was too small for the numbers that flocked to it; but the present truly Apostolic Bishop of Waterford, the Right Rev. Dr. Foran, when parish priest of Dungarvan, built a magnificent schoolhouse, and a residence for the Christian Brothers at his own expense; and there are no buildings in Ireland belonging to the order superior to them. In Cork the next foundation was laid; this was in 1811—and when we say that it was there that Gerald Griffin ended his days, we have said almost sufficient in praise of the noble institution of which that city boasts, and which is known as the Peacock Lane schools—presided over by a gentleman of the most extensive acquirements, and of the most solid piety and purest benevolence. In 1812 an establishment was founded in Dublin, where the order made unexampled progress, and where Mr. Rice lived for years, at the house in Townsend Street.

In 1815 the Most Rev. Dr. Bray introduced the order to Thurles, where the establishment flourishes admirably, doing incalculable service. The Right Reverend Dr, Thohy introduced the order in Limerick in 1816, and on the 5th of September, 1820, the bull of Pope Pius VII was issued confirming the institute as a religious order. Mr. Rice was elected to the office of superior-general on the 12th of January, 1822, after a retreat conducted by the late distinguished, learned, and apostolic Dr. Peter Kenny, S.J., whose family resided in Waterford, where his brother was for many years at the head of one of the most respectable medical establishments in the south of Ireland. At the end of ten years the Pope's brief having provided that a general chapter should be held at the end of every ten years, and that the superior-general should govern for ten years only, Mr. Rice was re-elected to the high office he had held, in January, 1833, at a chapter convened at the house of the order, North Richmond Street. Dublin. This establishment is one of the principal of the society, and may be said to have been the offspring of the Catholic Association—the foundation stone having been laid by the illustrious O'Connell in June, 1828, surrounded by a vast multitude, who walked in procession from the Corn Exchange to witness the ceremony. This house, from its opening in 1831, became the principal residence of Mr. Rice for the remainder of his official life, and if anything more than wanting to add to its celebrity as an educational establishment, it would be found in the fact—that it was to this retreat of society and learning that Gerald Griffin repaired in 1838, and entered as a novice among the Christian brothers.

In July, 1838 Mr. Rice resigned his office of superior, years and infirmities pressing hard upon him; and we may say that since that period he withdrew himself almost entirely from the cares in which he had been so long engaged, and devoted himself with pious assiduity to those more sublime concerns to which he ever attended, and of the necessity of which his life was a constant example to others. There are eleven houses of the order in Ireland. twelve in England, one in Sydney, and the applications for their extension to the colonies and other parts of Great Britain and Ireland are constant and unremitting. We have thus hastily sketched an imperfect outline of the life of this great and good man. Mr. Rice enjoyed the intimate friendship of many of the Catholic prelates of Ireland and England, and of the leaders of the Catholic body in both countries. He and the Liberator were always on terms of the most sincere esteem and respect. His masculine mind—his undaunted energy—his integrity and perserverance, were qualities which won admiration at the hands of all who came into contact with him. He was trustee of several charities. The bequests left to his own institution were numerous and munificent: and there can be no doubt but that the best possible use has been made of them. Well may he say—

'Ezegl monumentum aere perennius.'

He first laid the foundation of an educational system for the children of the Catholic poor of Ireland. On many and many a man, born in poverty, and who might have been brought up in crime, has he been instrumental of, not only , rescuing from peril, but affording the means of arriving at eminence in the merchantile world, and perhaps, in the learned professions. To his order he was a solid example of every virtue—to the community at large he was the same On all hands he was a Christian man in the most perfect sense of the word, The city which gave him birth has given the same to other illustrious men; but there is not one among the roll, perhaps, more conspicuous for public usefulness than Edmond Ignatius Rice, who has just been called, in the fullness of venerable years to receive the reward of his labours in that kingdom after which he long sighed. His remains are laid it the cemetery at Mount Sion, Waterford, and may he rest in peace.

Notes

CHAPTER 1: SPRING

1 E.M. Johnston, *Eighteenth-Century Ireland* (Dublin, 1974), p. 11.
2 W. King, *The state of the Protestants of Ireland under the late King James' government* (Dublin, 1691), p. 292. For a recent survey of the penal laws see T. Bartlett, *The Fall and Rise of the Irish Nation: the Catholic Question 1690–1830* (Dublin, 1992) and S.J. Connolly, *Religion, Law and Power: the making of Protestant Ireland, 1660–1760* (Oxford, 1992).
3 S.J. Connolly, *Religion, Law and Power*, p. 263.
4 L.M. Cullen, 'Catholics under the penal laws' in *Eighteenth-Century Ireland* (1986), pp. 29–31.
6 Connolly, *Religion Law and Power*, p. 311; idem, Priests and People in Pre-Famine Ireland (Dublin, 1981), p. 27. D. Dickson, 'Catholics and trade in eighteenth-century Ireland' in T. Power and K. Whelan (eds), *Endurance and Emergence: Catholics in Eighteenth-Century Ireland* (Dublin, 1990), pp. 85–100. Cullen, 'Catholic social classes' in Power and Whelan (eds), *Endurance and emergence*, pp. 57–84.
6 R.E. Burns, 'Irish Popery Laws: a study of eighteenth-century legislation and behavious', *Review of Politics* (1962): M. Wall, 'Penal Laws', in G. O'Brien (ed.) *Catholic Ireland in the Eighteenth-Century* (Dublin, 1989), p. 8: Bartlett, *Fall and Rise*, p. 19.
7 P.J. Corish, *The Catholic Community in the seventeenth and eighteenth centuries* (Dublin, 1981), p. 74.
8 1731 Report on the state of popery in *Arch. Hib.* (1913), pp. 146–51.
9 Connolly, *Religion, Law and Power*, p. 268.
10 M. Wall, 'The Penal Laws', in G.O'Brien (ed) *Catholic Ireland*, p. 7.
11 Bartlett, *Fall and Rise*, p. 26. Corish, *Catholic Community*, p. 163. I. Murphy, *The Diocese of Killaloe in the Eighteenth Century* (Dublin, 1992), p. 155.
12 Cited in P. Rogers, *The Irish Volunteers and Catholic Emancipation* (Dublin, 1934) p. 18.
13 For a recent study of Burke and Ireland see C. Cruise O'Brien, *The Great Melody* (London, 1993).
14 Rogers, *The Irish Volunteers*, p. 2. K. Whelan, The regional impact of Irish Catholicism 1700–1850' in W. Smyth and K. Whelan (eds), *Common Ground: essays in the historical geography of Ireland* (Cork, 1988) p. 254.
15 *Correspondence of Vicount Castlereagh*, IV (London, 1853), pp. 97–103.
16 Connolly, *Priests and People*, pp. 32–3.
17 Carrigan, *Ossory*, i, pp. 198–9 in F. O'Fearghail 'The Catholic Church in County Kilkenny 1600–1800' in W. Nolan and K. Whelan (eds) *Kilkenny: History and Society* (Dublin, 1990), p. 239.
18 Sweetman, Visitation diary 1753 in W.H. Grattan Flood, 'Diocesan manuscripts of Ferns during the reign of Bishop Sweetman' in Arch. Hib., II (1913), III (1914): P. Plunket, Visitation, Cogan (ed) *Diocese of Meath* (Dublin, 1993), iii, pp. 25–45.
19 Cogan, *Diocese of Meath*, iii, p. 38.
20 For an indication of the devotional material published in Cork alone, see H. Fenning, 'Cork imprints of Catholic historical interest 1723–1804: a provisional check-list' in *Jn. Cork Historical and Archaeological Society* (1995) pp. 129–48.
21 T. Wall, Archbishop Carpenter and the Catholic Revival' in *Reportorium Novum* (1955), pp. 178–9.

22 M. McGrath (ed), *The Diary of Humphrey O'Sullivan*, ii (Dublin, 1936), p. 183.

23 J. Troy, Schema for the diocesan clerical conference for 1790, Dublin Diocesan Archive.

24 Whelan, 'The regional impact of Irish Catholicism', p. 7.

25 A. McAuley, *Septennial parliaments vindicated* (Dublin, 1766), cited in Rogers, *Irish Volunteers*, p. 5.

26 K. Whelan, 'The Catholic Church in Tipperary, 1700–1900' in W. Nolan and T. McGrath (eds) *Tipperary: History and Society* (Dublin, 1985), pp. 225–7.

27 K. Whelan, 'The Catholic parish, the Catholic chapel and village development in Ireland' in *Irish Geography* (1983), pp. 1–16.

28 P. Power (ed.), 'A Carrickman's (James Ryan's) diary 1786–1809' *Waterford Arch. Soc. Jn* (1913), p. 19.

29 MacKenna to Antonneli, 20 March 1785, A.P.F., S.C. Irlanda, vol. 16, f.28; Jas Butler to Antonelli, 13 September 1784, A.P.F., S.C., Irlanda, vol. 16, fol. 132; F. Moylan to S.C. of the Council, 18 June 1785, A,P.F., S.O.C.G., vol. 871, f. 12 in P. O'Donoghue, 'The Catholic Church in Ireland in the Age of Revolution and Rebellion' (Ph.D., UCD, 1975), pp. 24–7; P. Corish, *The Irish Catholic Experience* (Dublin, 1985), p. 160.

30 T. Bartlett, 'The origins and progress of the Catholic Question in Ireland in Power and Whelan (eds), *Endurance and Emergence*, p. 8.

31 J. Hill, 'Religious toleration and the relaxation of the penal laws: an imperial perspective 1763–1780' in *Arch. Hib.* (1989), pp. 98–109

32 E. Burke to G. Nagle, 25 August 1778, *Burke Corr.* iii, pp. 18–20; T. Wyse, *Historical sketches of the late Catholic Association of Ireland*, i (Dublin, 1829), p. 101.

CHAPTER 2: CALLAN

1   For a discussion of eighteenth-century Callan, see J. Kennedy, 'Callan a corporate town 1700–1800' in Nolan and Whelan (eds), *Kilkenny: History and Society* (Dublin, 1990), pp. 289–304.

2   L.M. Cullen, 'The Hidden Ireland: reassessment of a concept' in *Studia Hib.*, ix (1969), pp. 7–47.

3   R. Chetwood, *A tour through Ireland in several entertaining letters* (Dublin, 1748), pp. 146–9 in Kennedy, 'Callan', p. 290.

4   W. Tighe, *Statistical observations relative to the county of Kilkenny made in 1800 and 1801* (Dublin, 1802), pp. 457, 460, 464.

5   Tighe, *Statistical observations*, p. 480

6   *Parliamentary Gazetteer of Ireland, 1844–45* (Dublin, 1845), i, p. 298.

7   McGrath (ed), *Diary of Humphrey O'Sullivan*, i, p. 45.

8   T. Power, 'Converts' in Power and Whelan (eds), *Endurance and Emergence*, pp. 101–129.

9   For an intriguing study of this survival see K. Whelan, 'An underground gentry? Catholic middlemen in the eighteenth century in *The Tree of Liberty: Radicalism, Catholicism and the construction of Irish identity 1760–1830* (Cork, 1995)

10 T. Power, *Land, politics and society in eighteenth-century Tipperary* (Oxford, 1993), p. 149.

11 K. Whelan, 'Gaelic Survivals' in the *Irish Review*, no. 7 (1989), p140.

12 Registry of Deeds, Will of Robert Rice, 1787; Applotment Book, Parish of Callan, 18/6/1827, applotment nos 358, 363, 364.

13 M.C. Normoyle (ed), *Memoirs of Edmund Rice* (Dublin, 1979), pp. 114, 138, 253.

14 Tighe, *Statistical observations*, p. 385.

15 Whelan 'Underground Gentry'.

16 L.M. Cullen, 'Catholic social classes', p. 62.

17 Normoyle (ed.), *Memoirs*, p218.

18 J.S. Donnelly, 'The Whiteboy movement, 1761–65', *I.H.S.* (1978), pp. 20–54.

19 P. Wallace, 'Archbishop James Butler II' in W. Nolan (ed) *Thurles: the cathedral town* (Dublin, 1989), pp. 47–54.

20 Kennedy, 'Callan', p. 293; J. Burtchaell and D. Dowling 'Social and economic conflict in

county Kilkenny 1600–1800' in Nolan and Whelan (eds), *Kilkenny*, pp. 251–73.
21 John Troy, *Pastoral and Excommunication* (Kilkenny, 1779)
22 F. O'Fearghail, 'Catholic Church in County Kilkenny', p. 229.
23 T.C. Butler, *The Augustinians in Callan, 1467–1977* (Kildare, 1977).
24 Carrigan, *Ossory*, iv, p. 404.
25 M.C. Normoyle, *A Tree is Planted* (Dublin, 1976), p. 10.
26 [M. McCarthy] A Christian Brother, *Edmund Ignatius Rice and the Christian Brothers* (Dublin, 1926), p. 51.
27 Tighe, *Statistical observations*, p. 515
28 [McCarthy], *Edmund Rice*, p. 49.

CHAPTER 3: MERCHANT

1 See J.E. Carroll, 'From Charism to Mission to Ministry: Edmund Rice and the founding years of the Christian Brothers' in *Edmund*, 10 (Rome, 1991), pp. 19–43.
2 C. Smith, *The Ancient and Present State of the County and City of Waterford* (Dublin, 1746), p. 195.
3 S. Lewis, *Topographical Dictionary of Ireland* (London, 1837), p. 687.
4 Wakefield, ii, p. 624
5 Normoyle, *Memoirs*, pp. 120, 175.
6 L.M. Cullen, *The Emergence of Modern Ireland 1600–1900* (Dublin, 1981), p. 126.
7 Whelan, 'Regional impact', pp. 258–62
8 [McCarthy], *Edmund Rice*, p. 67.
9 Normoyle, *Memoirs*, pp. 23, 26, 34.
10 Normoyle, *Memoirs*, p. 224.
11 [McCarthy], *Edmund Rice*, p. 55.
12 *Dublin Evening Post*, 17 January 1789
13 Normoyle, *A Tree is Planted*, p. 25.
14 L. Ó Caithnia, 'The Death of Mrs Edmund Rice' in P.S. Carroll (ed.), *A Man Raised Up* (Dublin, 1994), pp. 67–79.
15 Dorothea Herbert, *Recollections* (1770–1806) cited in î Caithnia, p. 73.
16 Ó Caithnia, p. 76.
17 Normoyle, *A Tree is Planted*, p. 28.
18 E. Rice to M.P. Keeshan, Presentation Convent, Waterford, n.d. [1836] in M.C. Normoyle (ed), *A companion to a Tree is Planted: the correspondence of Edmund Rice and his assistants 1810–1842* (Dublin, 1977), pp. 494–5.
19 A.L. O'Toole, *A spiritual profile of Edmund Ignatius Rice*, i (Bristol, 1984), p. 87.
20 Carroll, p. 21.
21 Carroll, p. 22.
22 Normoyle, *Memoirs*, p. 138.
23 Coppinger to Bishop Laffan, 11 October 1824 in D. Dickson, 'Catholics and trade in Eighteenth-Century Ireland' in Power and Whelan (eds), *Endurance and Emergence*, pp. 92–3.
24 Garrett Connolly to E. Rice, 6 Feb. 1820, in Normoyle, *Companion*, p. 55.
25 Fitzpatrick, *Edmund Rice*, p. 59
26 A. O'Neill, 'Nuns and Monks at Hennessy's Road', O'Carroll, *A Man Raised Up*, pp. 79–96.
27 [McCarthy] *Edmund Rice*, pp. 277–8; O'Connell, *Life of Charles Bianconi*, p. 36.
28 T.W. Tone, cited in D. Keogh, *The French Disease: the Catholic Church and Irish radicalism, 1790–1800* (Dublin, 1993), pp. 55–6.
29 R. Dudley Edwards (ed), 'The minute book of the Catholic Committee, 1779–92', *Arch. Hib.*, ix (1942), pp. 157–60.
30 *Waterford Herald*, 8 May 1792.

31   *Waterford Herald*, 10 April 1793; 31 January 1795
32   Letter of Br Austin Dunphy, 21 June 1846, C.B.'s General Archives, Rome, Normoyle, *A Tree is Planted*, p. 23.
33   Keogh, *French Disease*, p. 176.

CHAPTER 4: DECISION

1   T. Corcoran, 'Enforcing the penal code on education', *Irish Monthly*, lx (1931), pp. 149–54.
2   P.J. Dowling, *Hedge Schools of Ireland* (Dublin, 1933).
3   M.E. Daly, 'The development of the National School system, 1831–40' in A. Cosgrove (ed), *Studies in Irish History Presented to R. Dudley Edwards* (Dublin, 1979), pp. 150–63.
4   E. Cahill, 'The Native Schools of Ireland in the Penal Era', *Irish Ecclesiastical Record* (1940), p. 21.
5   H. Fenning (ed), 'John Kent's report on the state of the Irish mission, 1742', *Arch. Hib* (1966), pp. 59–102; Corish, *Catholic Community*, p. 79.
6   I. Murphy, *The Diocese of Killaloe in the Eighteenth-Century* (Dublin, 1991), p 156.
7   Cahill, 'Native schools', p. 22.
8   Daly, 'National Schools', p. 154.
9   E. Rice to De la Salle Superior, Paris, 19 August 1826, Normoyle, *Companion*, p. 159.
10   D. Keogh, 'Thomas Hussey, Bishop of Waterford and Lismore 1797–1803 and the rebellion of 1798' in Nolan and Power (eds), *Waterford*, pp. 403–26.
11   J. Healy, *Centenary History of Maynooth* (Dublin, 1895).
12   W.G. Murphy, 'The life of Dr Thomas Hussey (1746–1803), Bishop of Waterford and Lismore' (Unpublished M.A. thesis, U.C.C, 1968), p. 145.
13   T. Hussey to E. Burke, 9 May 1797, *Burke Corr.*, iv, pp. 444–6.
14   T. Hussey, *A pastoral letter to the Catholics of the united dioceses of Waterford and Lismore* (Waterford, 1797).
15   Hussey, *Pastoral*, p. 3.
16   T. Tickle, *A letter to the Rev. Dr Hussey* (Dublin, 1797), p. 1.
17   P. Duigenan, *A fair representation of the present political state of Ireland* (London, 1799), p. 20; O'Beirne to Castlereagh, 27 April 1799, in Castlereagh Corr, ii, p. 283: J. Troy to T. Bray, 15 April 1797, Cashel Diocesan Archives.
18   Fitzpatrick, *Edmund Rice*, p. 85.
19   Fr Fitzgerald, 1 October 1844 in J. Shelly, *Edmund Ignatius Rice and the Christian Brothers* (Kilkenny, 1863), p. 42.
20   Fitzpatrick, *Edmund Rice*, p. 95.
21   [McCarthy] *Edmund Rice*, p. 70.
22   Statement of Br Bernard Dunphy begfore the Commissioners of the Primary Education Inquiry, 1825, Normoyle, *A tree is planted*, p. 39.
23   C. Clear, *Nuns in nineteenth-century Ireland* (Dublin, 1985) p. 49.
24   A. O'Neill, 'Nuns and Monks at Hennessy's Road', p. 86.

CHAPTER 5: BEGINNINGS

1   Hussey to Burke, 9 May 1979, *Burke Corr.*, ix, pp. 444–6.
2   Registry of Deeds, Dublin, 715, 145, 489080, Normoyle, *A Tree is Planted*, pp. 437–8.
3   Carroll, 'Charism to Mission', p. 23.
4   Corcoran, *Selected Texts*, p. 110
5   Normoyle, *Memoirs*, p. 197.
6   [McCarthy] *Edmund Rice*, p. 80.
7   Registry of Deeds, No. 553–315–368721, Normoyle, *A Tree is Planted*, p. 46.
8   *Christian Brothers' Educational Record* (Dublin, 1891), p. 447.
9   *Christian Brothers' Educational Record* (1891), p. 447.
10   T. Hearn to Donoughmore, Public Record Office of Northern Ireland, T3459/D34/1.

11 Will of Thomas Hussey in *Arch. Hib.*, iii (1914), p. 201.
12 Thomas Hussey, *Relatio Status*, 29 June 1803, S.C.R.I., 1802–1810, vol. 18, fol. 125.
13 Cited in [McCarthy], *Edmund Rice*, p. 72.
14 *The Dublin Pilot*, 23 March 1836.
15 Normoyle (ed), *Memoirs*, p. 13.
16 H.D. Inglis, *Ireland in 1834: a journey throughout Ireland, in the spring, summer and autumn of 1834*, ii (London, 1834), pp. 65–6.
17 *Practical observations on the First Report of the Commissioner on Irish Education* [1825], Normoyle, *A Tree is Planted*, p. 59.
18 R.H. Ryland, *History, Topography and Antiquities of Waterford* (London, 1824), p. 187; J. Newport to Melbourne, 1829, in Normoyle, *A Tree is Planted*, p. 59.
19 [McCarthy] *Edmund Rice*, p. 88.

CHAPTER 6: EXPANSION

1 J.A. Froude, *The English in Ireland in the Eighteenth-Century*, iii (New York, 1888), p. 54.
2 Power (ed), 'Carrickman's (James Ryan's) Diary', *Waterford Arch. Soc. Jn* (1913), p. 19.
3 See M.C. Sullivan, *Catherine McAuley and the Tradition of Mercy* (Dublin, 1995); D. Forristal, *The First Loreto Sister* (Dublin, 1994).
4 Whelan, 'Regional impact', p. 268.
5 Fitzpatrick, *Edmund Rice*, p. 158.
6 Whelan, 'Regional impact', p. 269.
7 Inglis, *Ireland in 1834*.
8 Power (ed), 'Carrick Man's Diary' (1913), p. 26.
9 Whelan, 'Catholic Church, 1700–1900' in Power and Nolan (eds), *Tipperary: History and Society*, p. 231.
10 Christian Brothers House Annals, Carrick-on-Suir, Normoyle, *A Tree is Planted*, p. 68.
11 The most recent Confirmations before that were held in 1791, Power, 'Carrickman's Diary' (1913), p. 75.
12 Hussey to Propaganda Fide, 29 June 1803, SRCI, 1802–10, Vol. 18, F. 125 in Normoyle (ed), *The Roman Correspondence* (Dublin, 1978), p. 3.
13 FitzPatrick, *Edmund Rice*, p. 160.
14 Normoyle, *A Tree is Planted*, p. 70.
15 Bartlett, *Fall and Rise*, p. 289 ff.
16 Memorial to Holy See in Favour of the Institute founded by Edmund Rice, 21 Jan. 1809, SRCI, 1808–09, Vol. 18, F. 495 Propaganda Fide to Dr Power, 21 Jan. 1809, LDSC, 1806–13, Vol. 294, F. 94–5; Normoyle, *Roman Correspondence*, pp. 4–8.
17 Normoyle, *A Tree is Planted*, p. 88.
18 *Christian Brothers Education Record* (1901), p. 532.
19 FitzPatrick, *Edmund Rice*, p. 292.
20 O'Toole, *A Spiritual Profile of Edmund Rice*, i, p. 58.
21 *History of the Institute*, i, p. 392.
22 E. Rice to Bray, 9 May 1810, C.D.A., in Normoyle (ed), *Companion*, p. 1.
23 Rev. John England (1786–1842), in [McCarthy] *Edmund Rice*, p. 106.
24 W. Meagher, *Notes on the life and character of His Grace, Most Rev. Daniel Murray* (Dublin, 1853), p. 146.
25 Rev. Fr Lynch, 1864, in [McCarthy] *Edmund Rice*, p. 115.
26 *Parliamentary Gazette*, cited in J.E. Carroll, 'From Charism to Mission', p. 37.
27 *Christian Brothers Education Record* (1909), p. 54.
28 Normoyle, *A Tree is Planted*, p. 158.
29 E. Rice to Fr Dunn, Preston, 24 June 1825, Normoyle, *Companion*, pp. 116–17.
30 *Christian Brothers' Education Record* (1894), p. 469.

CHAPTER 7: STRIFE

1 S.J. Connolly, 'Mass politics and sectarian conflict, 1823–30' in W.E. Vaughan (ed), *New History of Ireland*, v (Oxford, 1989), p. 75.
2 R. Musgrave, *Memoirs of the different rebellions in Ireland* (Reprinted, Wexford, 1995).
3 I. Murphy, 'Some attitudes to religious freedom and ecumenism in pre-emancipation Ireland' in *Irish Ecclesiastical Record* (1966), pp. 97–9.
4 S.J. Connolly, *Religion and Society in nineteenth-century Ireland* (Dundalk, 1985), pp. 25–30.
5 Cited in Murphy, 'Attitudes', p. 104.
6 See J. Liechty, 'The popular reformation comes to Ireland: the case of John Walker and the foundation of the Church of God 1804' in R.V. Comerford (ed.), *Religion, Conflict and Co-existence in Ireland* (Dublin, 1990), pp. 159–87.
7 Cited in D. Hempton and M. Hill, *Evangelical Protestantism in Ulster Society 1740–1890* (London, 1992), p. 53.
8 G. Taylor, *A history of the rise, progress and suppression of the rebellion in the county of Wexford in the year 1798* (Dublin, 1800), p. 99.
9 D. Hempton, 'The Methodist Crusade in Ireland, 1795–1845', *IHS* (1980), p. 36.
10 Hempton, 'Methodist Crusade', p. 33.
11 W.J. Amherst, *The history of Catholic emancipation 1771–1820* (London, 1886), i, p. 147, cited in Hempton, 'Methodist Crusade', p. 34.
12 *Report of the proceedings of a meeting in Cavan ... January 1827 to form a society for promoting the reformation in Ireland* (Cork, 1827), p. 17; Pastoral Address of Dr Touhy, *D.E.P.*, 3 July 1824.
13 Bartlett, *Fall and Rise*, p. 320.
14 Daly, 'National Schools', p. 154.
15 *D.E.P.*, 27 April 1824 in Murphy, 'Attitudes', p. 101.
16 Murphy, 'Attitudes', p. 101.
17 Fitzpatrick, *Edmund Rice*, pp. 231–6.
18 Dr O'Shaughnessy to E. Rice, 31 March 1826, Normoyle, *Companion*, p. 136.
19 Dean Shaughnessy, Ennis, 26 Dec. 1826 to E. Rice, *Normoyle* (ed), Companion, p. 164.
20 Dean Shaughnessy, Ennis, 16 Jan. 1827 to E. Rice, *Normoyle* (ed), Companion, p. 165.
21 D.V. Kelleher, 'A timely restorer of faith and hope in Ireland', in Carroll (ed), *A Man Raised Up*, p. 108.
22 Cited in Normoyle, *A Tree is Planted*, p. 61.
23 J.E. Gordon cited in Normoyle, *A Tree is Planted*, p. 62.
24 E. Rice to P. Kenney S.J., 11 May 1814, Normoyle, *Companion*, p. 17.
25 Troy to Rome, [3 June 1818?], SORCG, 1821, Vol. 926, Pt. 2, F. 146–8, in Normoyle, *Roman Correspondence*, p. 19.
26 Walsh to Propaganda, 30 July 1818, SRCI, Vol. 21, F. 354–5, in Normoyle, *Roman Correspondence*, p. 23.
27 Objection of Six Monks, 1 August 1818, SRCI, 1818, Vol. 21, F. 414, Normoyle, *A Tree is Planted*, pp. 118–19.
28 17 Pastors of the diocese of Waterford, 11 Sept. 1818, SRCI, Vol. 21, F. 513, Normoyle, *Roman Correspondence*, pp. 28–30. B. Coldrey, *Faith and Fatherland* (Dublin, 1988), p. 24.
29 Normoyle, *A Tree is Planted*, p. 120.
30 Fitzpatrick, *Edmund Rice*, p. 182.
31 Fontana to Bishops of Ireland, 18 Sept. 1818, cited in Fitzpatrick, *Edmund Rice*, p. 183.
32 Murray to Edmund Rice, 3 October 1820, Normoyle, *Companion*, p. 66.
33 D.S. Blake, *A Man for our time: a short life of Edmund Rice* (Dublin, 1994), p. 13.
34 *Presentation Record* (1918), in D.H. Allen, *The Presentation Brothers*, I (Cork, 1993), p. 51.

CHAPTER 8: EMANCIPATION?

1 D. O'Herlihy et al (eds), *To the cause of liberality: a history of the O'Connell Schools and the Christian Brothers, North Richmond Street* (Dublin, 1995), p. 16.

2 Bartlett, *Fall and Rise*, p. 329.
3 Connolly, 'Mass politics', p. 84.
4 Bartlett, *Fall and Rise*, p. 332.
5 Cited in Hempton, 'Methodist Crusade', p. 39.
6 *Freeman's Journal*, 10 June 1828.
7 [McCarthy], *Edmund Rice*, p. 269.
8 Connolly, *Religion and Society*, p. 28.
9 Letter of Br Austin Grace, 13 July 1875, C.B., General Archives, Rome, Normoyle, *A Tree is Planted*, p. 214.
10 Br J. Leonard to Fr Pius Leahy OP, 21 November 1829, Normoyle (ed), *Companion*, p. 213.
11 Normoyle, *A Tree is Planted*, p. 215.
12 10 George IV c. 7, XXVI – XXXVII.
13 Hansard, *House of Lords*, 2 April 1829, p. 56.
14 *History of the Institute*, i, p. 141.
15 Rice to Duke of Wellington, 6 April 1829 cited in R. Walsh, 'A list of the regulars registered in Ireland pursuant to the Catholic Relief Act of 1829', *Arch. Hib.*, iii (1914), p. 48.
16 Leahy, 28 March 1829, cited in Walsh, 'List of Regulars', p. 40.
17 O'Connell to H. O'Meara, Cork, 18 March 1829, *History of the Institute*, i, p. 139.
18 Cited in Fitzpatrick, *Edmund Rice*, p. 223.
19 Blake, *Short Life*, p. 16.
20 'J K.L.', *Letters on the State of Ireland* (Dublin, 1825), p. 19, cited in Hempton and Hill, *Evangelical Protestantism*, p. 55.
21 Daly, 'National Schools', p. 152.
22 Speech of Daniel O'Connell to the A.G.M. of the Society for the Promotion of the Education of the Poor in Ireland, 24 February 1820, cited in A. Hyland and K. Milne (eds), *Irish Educational Documents*, i (Dublin, 1987), p. 89.
23 H. Hislop, 'The 1806–12 Board of Education and non-denominational education in Ireland', *Oideas* (1993), pp. 48–61.
24 For this and subsequent discussion of the System I rely on Daly, 'National System' and I. Murphy, 'Primary Education', *A History of Irish Catholicism*, v, pp. 1–33.
25 *Freeman's Journal*, 9 May 1832, cited in Murphy, 'Primary Education', p. 13.
26 Stanley to Murray, 25 February 1831.
27 Daly, 'National Schools', p. 156.
28 Hislop, 'Board of Education', p. 48.
30 Blake, *Short life*, p. 17.
31 *Christian Brothers' Education Record*, 1895, p. 411.
32 Murphy, 'Primary Education', p. 9. G. Balfour, *Educational Systems*, p. 92 cited in Dowling, *History of Irish Education* (Cork, 1971), p. 122.
33 *Fifth Book of Lessons* (Dublin, 1836), p. 199.
34 *Fourth Book of Lessons* (Dublin, 1850), pp. 52–6. See R.J. Scally, *The End of Hidden Ireland: rebellion, famine and emigration* (Oxford, 1995).
35 D.H. Akenson, 'Pre-University Education, 1782–1870' in Vaughan, *New History of Ireland*, v, p. 532.
36 *Powis Commission Report*, Vol. III, p. 83, Letter of Br J.A. Hoare, Normoyle, *A Tree is Planted*, pp. 280–81.
37 Rice to D. Murray, 4 June 1837, D.D.A.

CHAPTER 9: AUTUMN

1 [McCarthy], *Edmund Rice*, pp. 399–400.
2 E. Rice's circular letter, 22 January 1838, Normoyle, *Companion*, pp. 515–16.
3 Normoyle, *A Tree is Planted*, p. 311.

4   Memoir of Brother Stephen Carroll, Normoyle, *Companion*, p. 42.
5   Memoir of Brother Stephen Carroll, Normoyle, *Companion*, p. 44
6   Normoyle, *A Tree is Planted*, p. 320.
7   Blake, *Edmund Rice*, p. 19.
8   Normoyle, *A Tree is Planted*, p. 348.
9   E. Rice to D. Murray, 14 Sept. 1840, Normoyle, *Companion*, pp. 551–2.
10 Petition to the Holy See against Br Michael Paul Riordan, 30 July 1840, Normoyle, *Roman Correspondence*, pp. 207–11.
11 Kenney to D. Murray, 31 December 1840, Normoyle, *A Tree is Planted*, p. 358.
12 M.P. Riordan to P. Cullen, 15 Nov. 1842, Normoyle, *Roman Correspondence*, p. 329.
13 [McCarthy], *Edmund Rice*, p. 416.
14 Normoyle, *Memoirs*, p. 16.
15 Normoyle, *A Tree is Planted*, p. 407.
16 Normoyle, *A Tree is Planted*, p. 407.
17 [McCarthy], *Edmund Rice*, p. 416.
18 Normoyle, *A Tree is Planted*, p. 409.
19 [McCarthy], *Edmund Rice*, p. 418.
20 Br J. Murphy to Commissioners of Charitable Donations and Bequests, 11 September 1844, cited in Normoyle, *A Tree is Planted*, p. 413.
21 [McCarthy], *Edmund Rice*, p. 419.
22 Carried in *The Tipperary Vindicator*, 4 September 1844.
23 Oration of Fr R. Fitzgerald, 1 Oct. 1844, cited in [McCarthy], *Edmund Rice*, p. 429.

CHAPTER 10: MODERNISATION

1   E. Rice to P. Kenney, S.J., 11 May 1814, Normoyle, *Companion*, pp. 17–19; Carroll, *From Christian Mission* , p. 23.
2   Whelan, 'Regional impact', p. 267.
3   S. Smiles, *Men of Invention and Industry* (London, 1844), cited in [McCarthy], *Edmund Rice*, pp. 66–7.
4   *Waterford Chronicle*, 29 June 1816, in Normoyle, *A Tree is Planted*, p. 61.
5   Ryland, *History* (Waterford, 1824), pp. 187–8.
6   Rice to T. Bray, 9 May 1810, Normoyle, *Companion*, p. 5. House Annals, Carrick-on-Suir, 1814, Normoyle, *A Tree is Planted*, p. 55.
7   [McCarthy], *Edmund Rice*, p. 88.
8   H.F. Kearney, 'Fr Mathew: Apostle of Modernisation' in A. Cosgrove (ed.), *Studies in Irish History*, pp. 164–175.
9   Thackery, *Irish Sketch Book*, cited in M. Lysaght, *Fr Theobald Mathew: the Apostle of Temperance* (Dublin, 1983).
10 Kearney, 'Fr Mathew', p. 175.
11 C. Kerrigan., *Father Mathew and the Irish Temperance Movement, 1838–1849* (Cork, 1992). Lysaght, *Fr Mathew*, p. 32.
12 FitzPatrick, *Edmund Rice*, p. 280.
13 Normoyle, *Memoirs*, p. 111.
14 Normoyle, *Memoirs*, p. 17.
15 Fr Augustine, *Fr Mathew and Edmund Rice*, p. 11.
16 Fr Augustine, *Fr Mathew and Edmund Rice*, p. 20.
17 Fr Augustine, *Fr Mathew and Edmund Rice*, p. 23.
18 Fr Augustine, *Fr Mathew and Edmund Rice*, p. 29.
19 Fr Augustine, *Fr Mathew and Edmund Rice*, p. 26.
20 E. Rice to B. Bolger, 10 August 1810, Normoyle, *Companion*, p. 7.
21 J. McQuaid, Foreword, Fitzpatrick, *Edmund Rice*, p. x.
22 I am grateful to Br Michael Murray for bringing this to my attention.

Bibliography

PRIMARY SOURCES: PRINTED

Christian Brothers' Education Record (1891, in progress).

Normoyle, M.C.(ed), *A Companion to a Tree is Planted: the correspondence of Edmund Rice and his Assistants, 1810–1842* (Dublin, 1977)

— *The Roman Correspondence: treating of the early years of the Institute of Edmund Rice 1803–1844* (Dublin, 1979).

— *Memoirs of Edmund Rice* (Dublin, 1979)

SECONDARY SOURCES

Akenson, D.H., *A Protestant in Purgatory: Richard Whateley Archbishop of Dublin* (Conn., 1981)

Atkinson, N., *Irish Education: A history of educational Institutions* (Dublin, 1969).

Augustine, Fr, *Edmund Ignatius Rice and Theobald Mathew* (Dublin, 1944).

Bartlett, T., *The Fall and Rise of the Irish Nation: The Catholic Question 1690–1830* (Dublin, 1992).

Blake, D., *A Man for our times: a short life of Edmund Rice* (Dublin, 1994).

Bowen, D., *The Protestant Crusade in Ireland 1800–70: a study of Protestant–Catholic relations between the Act of Union and Disestablisment* (Dublin, 1978).

Burtchael, J. and Dowling, D., 'Social and economic conflicts in county Kilkenny, 1600–1800' in W. Nolan and K. Whelan(eds), *Kilkenny: History and Society* (Dublin, 1990), pp. 251–72.

Cahill, E., 'The native schools of Ireland in the penal era', *Irish Ecclesiastical Record* (1940), pp. 16–28.

Carroll, J.E., 'From Christian Mission to Ministry: Edmund Rice and the Founding Years of the Christian Brothers' in *Edmund* (Rome, 1991), pp. 19–43.

Carroll, S . (ed), *A Man Raised Up: Recollections and Reflections on Venerable Edmund Rice* (Dublin, 1994).

Clear, C., *Nuns in Nineteenth-Century Ireland* (Dublin, 1985).

Colrey, B.M., *Faith and Fatherland: The Christian Brothers and the development of Irish Nationalism, 1838–1821* (Dublin, 1988).

Connolly, S.J., *Religion and Society in Nineteenth-Century Ireland* (Dundalk, 1988).

— *Religion, Law and Power: the making of Protestant Ireland 1660–1760* (Oxford, 1992).

— 'Religion, work, discipline and economic attitudes; the case of Ireland', in T.M. Divine and D. Dickson(eds), *Ireland and Scotland 1600–1850* (Edinburgh, 1983), pp. 235–47.

Corish, P., *The Catholic Community in the Seventeenth and Eighteenth Centuries* (Dublin, 1981).

Cullen, L.M., 'Catholics under the penal laws' in *Eighteenth-Century Ireland* (1986), pp. 23–36.

— 'The Hidden Ireland: reassesment of a concept' in *Studia Hib.*, ix (1969), pp. 7–47.

— *The Emergence of Modern Ireland, 1600–1900* (Dublin, 1983).

Daly, M., 'The Development of the National School System, 1831–40', in A. Cosgrove and D. McCartney (eds), *Studies in Irish History Presented to R. Dudley Edwards* (Dublin, 1979), pp. 150–63.

Dickson, D., 'Catholics and trade in eighteenth-century Ireland', in T. Power and K. Whelan (eds), *Endurance and Emergence* (Dublin, 1990), pp. 185–200.

Dowling, P.J., *A history of Irish education: a study in conflicting loyalties* (Cork, 1971).

FitzPatrick, J.D., *Edmund Rice* (Dublin, 1945).

Hempton, D., 'The Methodist Crusade in Ireland 1795–1845, *Irish Historical Studies* (1980), pp. 33–48.

— with Hill, M., *Evangelical Protestantism in Ulster Society, 1740–1890* (London, 1992).

Hislop, H., 'The 1806–12 Board of Education and non-denominational education in Ireland', *Oideas*, (1993), pp. 48–61.

Kearney, H.F., 'Father Mathew: Apostle of Modernisation' in A. Coscgove and D. McCartney (eds), *Studies in Irish History Presented to R. Dudley Edwards* (Dublin, 1979), pp. 164–75.

Kennedy, J. 'Callan—a corporate town 1700–1800' in W. Nolan and K. Whelan (eds), *Kilkenny: History and Society* (Dublin, 1990), pp. 289–305.

Kerrigan, C., *Father Mathew and the Irish Temperance Movement, 1838–1849* (Cork, 1992).

Keogh, D., *The French Disease: the Catholic Church and Radicalism in Ireland 1790–1800* (Dublin, 1993).

— 'Thomas Hussey, Bishop of Waterford and Lismore, 1797–1803' in W. Nolan et al (eds), *Waterford: History and Society* (Dublin, 1992), pp. 403–26.

Liechty, J., 'The popular reformation comes to Ireland: the case of John Walker and the foundation of the church of God 1804' in R.V. Comerford et al (eds), *Religion, Conflict and Co-existence in Ireland* (Dublin, 1990), pp. 159–87.

Lysaght, M., *Fr Theobald Mathew: the Apostle of Temperance* (Dublin, 1983).

[Mc Carthy, M.], A Christian Brother, *Edmund Ignatius Rice and the Christian Brothers* (Dublin, 1926).

McGrath, T.G., 'The Tridentine Evolution of Modern Irish Catholicism, 1565–1962: a re-examination of the 'Devotional Revolution Thesis'' in R. O'Muiri (ed), *Irish Church History Today* (Armagh, 1990), pp. 84–100.

Murphy, I. 'Some attitudes to religious freedom and ecumenism in pre-emancipation Ireland, *Irish Ecclesiastical Record* (1966), pp. 93–104.

— *The Diocese of Killaloe in the Eighteenth-Century* (Dublin, 1992).

Normoyle, M.C., *A Tree is Planted: The Life and Times of Edmund Rice* (Dublin, 1976).

O'Herlihy, D. (ed), *To the Cause of Liberality: A history of the O'Connell Schools and the Christian Brothers, North Richmond Street* (Dublin, 1995).

O'Sullivan, M., *Charles Bianconi: A biography 1786–1875* (London, 1878)

O'Toole, A.L., *A Spiritual Profile of Edmund Rice*, 2 vols (Bristol, 1984).

Parkes, S., *Irish Education in the British Parliamentary Papers in the Nineteenth-Century* (Cork, 1978)

Quane, M., 'Waterford Schools in the opening decades of the nineteenth-century', *Royal Society of Antiquaries of Ireland* (1971), pp. 141–5.

Rushe, D. *Edmund Rice: the man and his times* (Dublin, 1981).

Shelly, J., *Edmund Ignatius Rice and the Christian Brothers: a compilation* (Kilkenny, 1863).

Sullivan, M.C., *Catherine McAuley and Tradition of Mercy* (Dublin, 1995).

Walsh, R., 'A list of the regulars registered in Ireland pursuant to the Catholic relief act of 1829' in *Arch. Hib*, iii (1914).

Whelan, K., Review article, 'Gaelic Survivals', in *The Irish Review* (1989), pp. 139–43.

— 'The regional impact of Irish Catholicism 1700–1850' in W. Smyth and K. Whelan (eds), *Common Ground: essays on the historical geography of Ireland* (Cork, 1988), pp. 253–77.

— *The tree of Liberty: Radicalism, Catholicism and the Construction of Irish Identity 1760–1830* (Cork, 1995).

Index